PAULINE PLACES

PAULINE PLACES

In the Footsteps of Paul through Turkey and Greece

Ronald Brownrigg

Hodder & Stoughton

LONDON SYDNEY AUCKLAND TORONTO

British Library Cataloguing in Publication Data

Brownrigg, Ronald
  Pauline places
  1. Bible N. T. Paul the Apostle, Saint. Local
  associations: Mediterranean region
  I. Title
  225.9'24

  ISBN 0-340-50401-3

Acknowledgments of Illustrations

Mr Philip Lyons, for Saga Holidays: 10, 11, 12, 13, 14, 15 and
   back cover
The Rev Dr Peter Bower: 5, 8, 9, 14
The Rev Cyril Mackenzie-Lowe: 5, 6, 7, 10
Mrs Rita Anelay: 4, 5, 6
Miss Kristine Gibbs: 8, 9, 15
Colonel Hugh Mackintosh: 2, 3
Canon John Hargreaves: 2, 3
Mr Brian Legg: 4 and front cover
Miss Barbara Spiller: 8, 12
The Rev Paul Conder: 3
Dr Raymond Anelay: 7
The Rev Kenneth Lawton: 1
Mr Richard Symes: 2

CONTENTS

PREFACE

I was privileged for a year to be Canon Ronald Brownrigg's curate when he was Rector of St Mary's Church Bletchingley, in Surrey. Often during that time I was left to run things whilst he went off leading pilgrimages to the Holy Land. I did not know at first hand how good he was at this business, though I had heard nothing but very good reports of his skill.

In 1988 after the Lambeth Conference, my wife and I and about thirty others from right round the world were greatly blessed to be led by Ron on a pilgrimage entitled, 'In the Footsteps of St Paul'. We visited Turkey and Greece. Ron was an outstanding leader giving us just enough information for us to savour the salient features of the sites but not so much as to stop us having a profound spiritual experience. I know because other pilgrims told us this; we were all greatly enriched by being led by a knowledgeable and caring pilgrimage guide.

Those who will read his latest book about the places sanctified by St Paul will realise that they are tapping a mine of valuable information preparing them to enjoy a great thrill when they do go on pilgrimage. He helps us open our eyes to see, and our ears to hear, even things of long ago as if we are experiencing contemporary events. And we cannot but be better for the experience, our faith comes alive so wonderfully on such occasions.

I commend this book warmly knowing that its readers are in for a great time.

The Most Reverend Desmond M. Tutu
Cape Town
27 December 1988

FOREWORD

As *Come, See the Place* sought to introduce the places and faces of the Gospels, so this little book seeks to do the same for the Epistles and the Book of Revelation. I dedicate it with gratitude to all those pilgrims who have kept me company during forty-seven years of travel to the Near East.

These pages are the fruit of journeys to all the places to which St Paul addressed his letters and to which he travelled in the Near East. I have also included others not mentioned by Paul or John the Divine, but which come within easy range of pilgrims visiting Pauline places and which they will not want to miss. Among these are Istanbul, where the traveller in transit to more distant Turkish destinations may need to change aircraft, also Hierapolis and Cappadocia, both of them set in unique scenery and natural phenomena.

All three have played an important part in the history of the Christian Church and faith. Also included are Patmos and three of the Seven Churches of Asia, more easily accessible and vividly illustrative of the opposition faced by Paul and John. Perhaps I might have included Smyrna of Polycarp, but that Greco-Roman city is buried beneath the bustling streets of modern Izmir and hard to discern for most pilgrims.

My hope is that many readers will come to see a journey 'In the Footsteps of St Paul' as a logical sequence to a visit to the Holy Land and, in the current political situation, rather more easy to arrange. If the Holy Land illuminates the Gospel for the day, the other will project the Epistle and Revelation in three dimensions.

Whether from your armchair or coach, you can travel with Paul along some Roman road, like that between Troas and Assos on the front cover (Acts 20:13). You can arrive with Paul, Barnabas or Silas or Luke, Timothy or Titus at some Greek or Galatian town, where you follow at once into the synagogue. He speaks loud enough to fill the prayer hall and reach out into the Gentiles' courtyard, where the 'God-fearers' gather and are held until sunset, when someone offers the strangers hospitality for the night.

It is in that magic moment that the Church in that township is planted within a household and survives Paul's often precipitate departure, through the faith and fidelity of the lady of the house. Again and again this happens: at Lystra it is Eunice, at Ephesus Claudia and Prisca, at Philippi Lydia, at Athens Damaris, at Corinth Chloe, at Cenchreae Phoebe – and so many more.

What was it that provoked this response? Paul's 'angelic' face (see page 5) or mercurial sermons (see page 73)? Yes perhaps, but as we discover on his journeys one of the most striking features of his ministry is his own personal physical stamina, together with his amazingly courageous disregard of his own personal suffering and corporal punishment. Who could reject such witness for the cross of Christ, both experienced and *lived* in the example of his Apostle Paul?

Today's pilgrims follow him by coach. *He* travelled by mule and on foot, often in rugged, mountainous terrain or on pirate-infested seas, some ten thousand miles in all. In the Holy Land, about the size of Wales, barely a hundred miles separates Nazareth and Galilee from Jerusalem and Bethlehem. Paul's second missionary journey alone covered nearly three thousand miles. As we seek to follow, we find these biblical sites far apart with long coach rides in between. It is then perhaps that the short chapters of this book may provide some preparation as we approach each place. It is on the actual site that each ground plan may show what is to be seen and where.

A good journey to all, with Paul, in Christ.

Ronald Brownrigg
Lent 1989

RIVER TIBER

ROME

NEAPOLIS

SICILY

RHEGIUM

SYRACUSE

MALTA

ILLYRICUM &
DALMATIA

MOESIA

SEA OF ADRIA

APPIAN WAY

MACEDONIA

THRACIA

PHILIPPI

EGNAT

THESSALONICA

ACHAIA

AEGEAN SEA

CORINTH

ATHENS

CENCHREAE

CRETE

FAIR HAVENS

MEDITERRANEAN SEA

CYRENE

The World of St. Paul

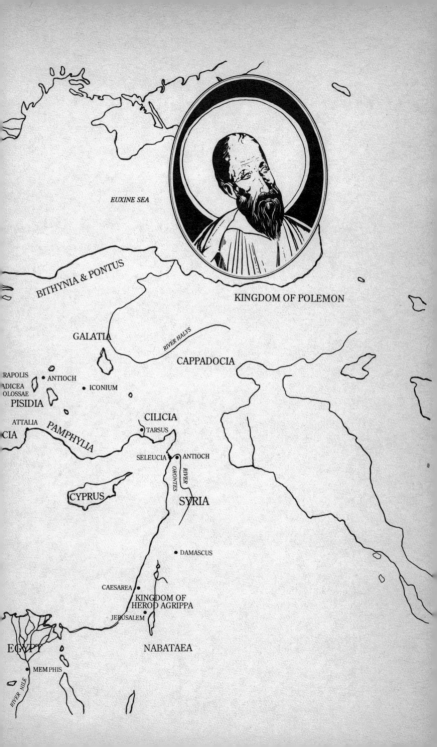

EUXINE SEA

KINGDOM OF POLEMON

BITHYNIA & PONTUS

GALATIA

RIVER HALYS

CAPPADOCIA

RAPOLIS
ADICEA   • ANTIOCH
OLOSSAE
PISIDIA   • ICONIUM

ATTALIA
CIA   PAMPHYLIA

CILICIA
• TARSUS

SELEUCIA • ANTIOCH

RIVER ORONTES

CYPRUS

SYRIA

• DAMASCUS

CAESAREA •

KINGDOM OF
HEROD AGRIPPA

JERUSALEM •

EGYPT   NABATAEA

• MEMPHIS

RIVER NILE

COLLECT

Almighty God,
who caused the light of the gospel
to shine throughout the world
through the preaching of your servant Saint Paul:
grant that we who celebrate his wonderful conversion
may follow him in bearing witness to your truth;
through Jesus Christ our Lord.

Part One:

FIRST-CENTURY SURVEY

PAUL THE PILGRIM

Lord Coggan records his own impression of the man Tarsus in his recent book, *Paul: Portrait of a Revolutionary* (Hodder & Stoughton, 1986):

I thought of him often as I recently covered some of the ground which he travelled in Turkey. True, the car which carried me seemed to have some of its parts held together with pieces of string, but we covered our distances with speed and with a measure of comfort. Paul travelled perhaps fifteen miles a day, 'in weariness and painfulness'. On my journey, I was impressed by the sheer beauty of the landscape. It was spring-time and the land was burgeoning with life. The peach trees were beginning to blossom – there was a haze of deep pink set off against a background of dark soil. The trees were budding – a filigree-work of yellowish-green as tender as the winter they had endured was long and hard. It was a land of apples, figs, grapes and nuts in rich abundance. The land which had silted up and strangled Ephesus and Miletus as ports was now a great alluvial plain, rich in crops, producing cotton in plenty. The variety of colour in the soils was enough to delight the heart of any artist, melting, sometimes, into a deep pink which seemed to reflect the complexion of some of the people themselves, whose dark skin looked as if a kindly brush had touched its surface with red. There were sheep and goats in plenty in Cilicia, constant reminders that it was with good reason that it had given its name to cilicium, the goat's hair which Paul, himself a tentmaker, had often used in his work.

Yet, for all the beauty and the plenty, there was a ferocity about the land where Paul undertook some of his most effective journeys. The Taurus Mountains are riven, scarred by fierce heat and bitter cold. The land is battered, weatherbeaten by the storms of long millennia. It can be no fun to be exposed to the ferocity of such weather. As Paul turned his back on the comforts of his one-time home, it must have called for superb endurance to expose himself to the furies of nature as he tramped from Tarsus to Iconium, to Hierapolis, to Ephesus, to Miletus . . . 'I have been constantly on the road; I have met dangers from rivers, dangers from robbers . . . dangers in the country, dangers at sea . . . I have toiled and drudged, I have often gone without sleep; hungry and thirsty, I have often gone fasting; and I have suffered from cold and exposure. I have suffered the loss of all things . . .' Endure hardness as a good soldier of Jesus Christ – this was a stark reality to the man of the city who tramped the country, weary mile after weary mile.

Tarsus today, between sea and Taurus Mountains, has much history but little evidence to show for it, from the time of Paul. In his own words, he was 'a Hebrew-speaking Jew of a Hebrew-speaking family, circumcised on my eighth day, Israelite by race, of the tribe of Benjamin, Hebrew born and bred; in my attitude to the law, a Pharisee; in pious zeal, a persecutor of the Church; in legal rectitude, faultless . . . thoroughly trained in every point of our ancestral law'.

His family at Tarsus was probably one of substance, held in high regard within Jewish Synagogue and Gentile university circles – with a sister and nephew living in Jerusalem. However rigid the family discipline, it would be impossible to protect young Paul from Greek culture, contact and games. It was not surprising that he should be attracted by the broad span of studies in the Gentile university, which at times even rivalled that of Athens. His time must have been divided between the discipline of the Synagogue and the naked exercise of the gymnasium – a combination of both Orthodoxy and Hellenism!

To discover 'what manner of man' Paul became, we need to 'soak in' the narratives of Acts and his own words of the Epistles, both in the original Greek and in modern translations. Early descriptions of Paul in maturity vary. One insists he had 'no presence and speech beneath contempt'. Another that he was 'short, bandy-legged, bald, blue-eyed, with eyebrows meeting over a large hooked nose – sometimes with the face of a man – sometimes with the face of an angel'. In later life, he was so scarred by constant punishment that the magistrates at Philippi needed only to see him stripped to be convinced of his criminality and guilt. To the end of his days on the Via Appia, he had only to raise a hand to silence the most aggressive crowd.

If he was an exact contemporary of Jesus, had he ever seen him? He claimed, 'Have I not seen Jesus?', but was he referring to his experience on the road to Damascus ('I am Jesus. You are persecuting me.') or to an experience at the foot of the cross? Certainly, Paul theologian and philosopher has inspired the writings of so many theologians down the centuries. The Damascus road experience has put a spark to so much tinder. The words of Paul have ignited in turn Augustine, Luther, Wesley, Barth, Hoskyns and countless others, who have shaped the faith of Europe. When theologians can be dead, Paul remains vividly alive – a man in love, 'in Christ' – his heart burning for Jesus.

Luke, in Acts, paints so well his courageous conviction and righteous anger in face of opposition. His own Epistles reveal his affection for his friends and congregations:
– When mercilessly flogged at Philippi and bundled without trial into prison, he demanded to be escorted out and through the city gate, by the very magistrates who had sentenced him.
– When standing before the sanhedrin at Jerusalem, the high priest Ananias ordered him to be hit across the mouth. Paul riposted with 'God will smite you, you

whited wall . . .' When those who stood by chided, 'How dare you speak to God's high priest like that?', he answered, 'I didn't realise it was God's high priest . . .' Was that just heavy irony, or did he in fact fail to see that it was the high priest? If the latter, was his 'thorn in the flesh' trachoma, rather than dysentery, malaria or epilepsy? That word 'skolops' implied the penetration of a sharp stake and the drag on the flesh of a fish-hook!

– And how he, Paul, resented Peter's playing the Pharisee and reverting to the imposition of dietary laws, over-turned by Christian faith. He felt that Peter not only 'with-drew' from such Christian family meals but ceremonially 'separated himself' in so doing – as he duly wrote to the Galatians, in a hot letter burning with correction.

– What pathos and affection when, after three years teaching at Ephesus, he calls the elders of that city to meet him at Miletus, for a harbour farewell!

– What love he shows, as 'mother and father' of his family at Corinth, as 'nurse' to the simple-hearted Thessalonians and as 'advocate' pleading and punning to Philemon for Onesimus, 'his own child begotten in prison'!

– What was it about Paul that called forth such response from the key women – mostly Gentiles – in each Christian community he founded?

– Nor was it in any false modesty that Paul called himself 'less than the least', as though the nearer he came to Jesus, the more aware he was of his lack of love.

– How he revelled in being the 'bond slave of the Christ' and the apostle/ambassador for Christ.

As we read and travel, may we meet Paul 'the Pilgrim' and become one with him to catch a glimpse of his charisma and vision. As we do so, we shall not be far from his Master, for they are inseparable.

> Yea, thro' life, death, thro' sorrow and thro' sinning
> He shall suffice me, for he hath sufficed.
> Christ is the end, for Christ is the beginning,
> Christ the beginning, for the end is Christ.
>
> F. W. H. Myers, 'St Paul'

2

PAUL, MAN OF THE ROAD

CONSTRUCTION

One of the most impressive achievements of the Romans was the vast network of roads, which they built to hold together their far-flung empire. The major roads were begun as early as the third century B.C., the Via Appia being completed by 312 B.C., only ten years after the death of Alexander the Great.

When constructing a road, the engineers dug a foundation trench three feet deep. They laid within this a foundation of sand, stones and concrete. On top of this they laid cobblestones in mortar; within the towns the cobblestones would be flat slabs, elsewhere irregular stones. Drainage channels carried away surplus rainwater. Stepping stones set across cobbled streets both slowed down the traffic and enabled pedestrians to cross the road dry. In Petra, Palmyra and Philippi, in Jerusalem and Jerash, the Roman streets are still scored with the scars and ruts of chariot wheels. In Jerash, as in other colonial cities, there are still tetrapylons at crossroads, sited like modern traffic lights at all four corners.

Some splendid viaducts and river bridges, too, still stand, including the Ponte Grosso on the Via Flaminia from Rome to Rimini and one bridge in Portugal 617 feet long, with arches ninety feet across.

All roads were measured from a golden milestone in the forum in Rome itself. The Roman mile – 140 yards short of

the English mile – measured 1,000 paces, from the Latin
(*mille*). Stone posts marked each mile. Some of these mile-
stones indicated cisterns, staging posts, rest-houses and
garrisons along the route.

NETWORK

From Rome, the Appian Way ran down to Naples (an early
Neapolis), where the road branched, one route continuing
south to Messina (on the toe of Italy), the other east to
Brindisi on the Adriatic (on the heel of Italy). This road was
fourteen to twenty feet wide – with room for two carriages
to pass side by side.

On the east of the Adriatic, opposite Brindisi, the Via
Egnatia ran from Apollonia eastwards across Macedonia to
reach the Aegean at Thessalonica. There, today, it runs
through the great Arch of Galerius in the centre of the
modern city and the Via Egnatia gives its name to the
east-west axis of the city. Just outside the Arch of Galerius
the Roman road, at right angles to the Egnatian Way, ran
south to Athens. This was the scene of Paul's decision not
to continue to Rome, but to turn south in his unsuccessful
mission to Athens. From Thessalonica, the Via Egnatia ran
100 miles east through the Roman garrison town of Philippi
to the port of Neapolis on the Aegean, whence it ran right
round to Constantinople – a total distance of 500 miles.
From Constantinople, the 'silk route' continued east
through Parthia to China, a further 1,000 miles through the
North-West Frontier Pass.

Some of the roads in Palestine go back to the Augustan
age – in Jerusalem through the Antonia Fortress gateway,
or the North Road down to the base port of Caesarea. The
greater part belong to the times of Trajan and Hadrian a
century later. The 'Street called Straight' in Damascus, the
'Via Recta', is still marked by Roman arches at each end and
indicates the east-west axis of the ancient city – some
thirteen feet below the present street level.

PURPOSE

This network of Roman roads was constructed with two purposes in mind:
1   To facilitate troop movements.
2   To serve the imperial postal service.
One accounts for the massive deployment and recall of legions from the centre to the outlying parts of the empire. *Two* was the Roman copy of the Persian 'pony express', inaugurated by Augustus. With staging posts and changes of horses every ten miles, and inns at twenty-five-mile intervals, couriers could average 120 miles a day.

For ordinary pedestrians, the average rate of travel was three miles per hour. Soldiers marched at four miles per hour, on forced marches rather more. The average distance on foot, covered in a day, of a pedestrian group would be between fifteen and twenty miles. A donkey or mule caravan would cover twenty, an individual carriage twenty-five to fifty miles a day at most.

Against such facts and figures, it is astonishing to note that the journeys of St Paul took him, in all, something over 12,000 miles. What an intrepid pioneer and tireless peripatetic – on foot or mule – he must have been, in a time of slow ships and fickle winds, in a rugged mountain terrain, infested with bandits and pirates! The extent of his stamina and courage can only be gauged against his physical condition. He was described as bandy-legged and his name (or nickname perhaps) was a term sometimes applied to the runt of the litter. But his greatest physical handicap was his constant 'thorn in the flesh', whatever that may have been – dysentery or trachoma or epilepsy or whatever. Only those who witnessed him stripped for flogging, over and over again, would grasp the cumulative effect of constant and debilitating physical punishment.

DRIVING FORCE

St Paul was essentially a man of the road – indeed of endless roads. The seed thoughts of all Paul's teaching are rooted in that personal encounter on the road to Damascus: 'I am Jesus. You are persecuting me'. Especially his doctrines of 'Grace' and of 'Justification by Faith'. So, too, the motive power of Paul's whole life springs from his philosophy of the cross. 'The Love of Christ constrains us and leaves us no choice', he writes (2 Corinthians 5:14). It certainly grasped and drove him on in an unending ministry of reconciliation of both Jews and Gentiles to God. He, Paul, came to know in himself the 'chemistry' of reconciliation. When the love and forgiveness of God for our selfish human nature conflicts with the wrath and justice of God, the inevitable consequence is the pain of God himself. In this reconciliation, Paul was proud to share saying: 'God forbid that I should glory save in the Cross of my Lord Jesus Christ, whereby I am crucified unto the world and the world is crucified unto me.'

Paul's Via Dolorosa, too, began from the Antonia Fortress, leading all the way to Rome, through triumphant pain, to his final re-creation – in the unfailing grace and power of the Risen Christ. What had begun on the road to Damascus was fulfilled on the road out of Rome.

3

ALL ROADS LEAD TO ROME

The imperial city was at the centre of a vast spider's web, a network of communications, to which the key was a policy of strategic colonisation, quite as purposeful as that of the British empire in the eighteenth and nineteenth centuries.

The thousands of Greek colonies all round the Mediterranean and Black Seas were mostly city settlements of Hellenes, driven overseas by the poverty of soil and broken terrain of their own peninsula. From the eighth and seventh centuries before Christ, courageous individuals and groups founded city states, politically independent from the host country, but inevitably commercially linked with their neighbours. For the most part, these colonies made no attempt to control the territory round them. They were transported communities seeking only the rights of guests on an alien coastline, but inevitably became cells of Greek culture in more primitive surroundings.

The Roman colony was an entirely different 'animal'. The *colonia* was a purposeful device of empire, a fragment of Rome with a body of Roman citizens, often demobilised veterans, designed to establish a bastion of Roman power in an unsettled countryside. Unlike the Greek colonies, the Roman were not necessarily new foundations, but were subdued or inherited, and sometimes troublesome problem areas – of which Galatia and Macedonia were typical. So Antioch in Pisidia, and Philippi at the terminus of the Via Egnatia postal route were 'national' Roman outposts of empire. Such ready-made frontier communities would be steadily 'Romanised', the most influential granted the coveted status of Roman citizenship and reinforced with immigrant citizens from Italy. Latin would be introduced for official announcements and inscriptions. Gradually, the Hellenic character of the city would be infiltrated until amusements, festivals, justice and even government had become Roman.

Paul of Tarsus was himself a Roman citizen who selected another, Silas, as his lieutenant. It would have been strange if Paul had *not* considered the imperial city as the final goal of his missionary ministry. For him, all roads had ultimately to lead to Rome. He takes decisive steps towards Roman communities and individuals, all along his journey to Rome. Those steps are often controversial and for Paul must have been at times very disappointing. On arrival in Cyprus, Paul and Barnabas landed at Salamis and went through the whole island to Paphos, seat of the Roman proconsul Sergius Paulus, whom Paul quickly converted. From that time, his own name was changed from 'Saul' to 'Paul'. On arrival in the Roman province of Galatia, he travelled directly north to the Roman colony of Antioch in Pisidia, to which he returned after visiting Iconium, Lystra and Derbe. He and Barnabas returned by sea to the Roman capital of the province of Syria, Antioch, 'Third City of the Empire', which was to become the headquarters of the Christian Missionary Movement.

As we associate Paul's loss of John Mark at the time of his decision to climb up to the Roman bastion of Pisidian Antioch, so we associate his gain of Luke at the time of his decision to cross the Aegean to Philippi, another great Roman colony. On his journey down to Thessalonica, he followed the Via Egnatia on its way to Rome, but for some reason of his own turned south – under the Arch of Augustus (later replaced by the present Arch of Galerius) and made for Athens and Corinth. With the exception of the events at Philippi, Paul was treated fairly by Roman officials. With effect from his arrest, three centurions in succession gave him protective custody – two at the

Antonia in Jerusalem and Julius, his escort on the journey to Rome, without whose respect and protection Paul would have been summarily executed during the shipwreck.

It is ironical that Paul reached his goal, the imperial city, under arrest and despite being under subsequent house arrest and imprisonment, was able to exercise a very considerable ministry through direct contact and through correspondence from Rome.

4

TABLE OF EVENTS AND LETTERS

Year	Outside Events	Events in Paul's Life	Letters Written	Reference
6 B.C.	Birth of Jesus			
10 A.D.?	Schooling in Nazareth	Birth of Paul		
		Schooling in Tarsus		
26	Galilean ministry of Jesus starts			
28		Rabbinic student in Jerusalem		
30	Crucifixion, Resurrection and Ascension of Jesus			
36	Pilate resigns procuratorship	Persecution of Hellenist Christians		Acts 7, 8
		Paul appointed to Damascus		Acts 9:4–19
		Conversion on road to Damascus		Gal. 1:17
	Stoning of Stephen	Retirement to Arabia. Return to		Gal. 1:17; Acts 9:20
	Aretas ruling Damascus	Damascus		Gal. 1:18; Acts 9:26
39	Herod Antipas exiled by Caligula	Visit to Jerusalem		Acts 9:30
		Return to Tarsus		
		Unrecorded mission to Syria and Cilicia		Gal. 1:21
44	Death of Herod Agrippa I	Assistant to Barnabas at Antioch		Acts 11:26
	Judea again a procuratorial province			
46		First Journey to Cyprus and Galatia, with Barnabas		Acts 13, 14

Date	Event	Journey/Events of Paul	Writings	Acts reference
48–53	Herod Agrippa II. Inspector of the Temple at Jerusalem			
49	Expulsion of Jewish-Christians from Rome by Claudius	Council of Jerusalem	Galatians (one theory)	Acts 15
50		Second Journey, with Silas to Europe	1 and 2 Thessalonians	Acts 16
51–2	Gallio at Corinth			Acts 18:12
52–60	Felix procurator of Judea	Return to Antioch, via Caesarea. Third Journey	Galatians (one theory)	Acts 18:22
53		Mission at Ephesus		Acts 19:1–20:1
54	Nero succeeds Claudius	Second Visit to Corinth; return via Troas and Miletus	1 and 2 Corinthians	
57		Arrival in Jerusalem	Romans	Acts 20; 21:1–14
58		Arrest and imprisonment at Caesarea		Acts 21:15 / Acts 21:27; 22; 23
		Trial before Felix		Acts 24
60	Festus succeeds Felix as procurator of Judea	Trial before Festus. Appeal to Caesar		Acts 25
		Appearance before Agrippa		Acts 26
		Departure for Rome		Acts 27
61–2		Winter on Malta, arrival at Rome		Acts 28:1–16
		Under house arrest in Rome	Colossians, Ephesians, Philemon, Philippians	Acts 28:16–31
62	Albinus succeeds Festus as procurator of Judea	Release and visit to perhaps Asia, Macedonia, Achaia, Spain	1 Timothy, Titus	
64–7	Nero's persecution of Christians in Rome	Re-arrest, perhaps in Troas	2 Timothy	2 Tim. 1:12; 4:13
		Imprisonment and execution in Rome		(Eusebius, 4th century)

NB The dating of all events and writings is approximate only.

OUTLINE OF JOURNEYS

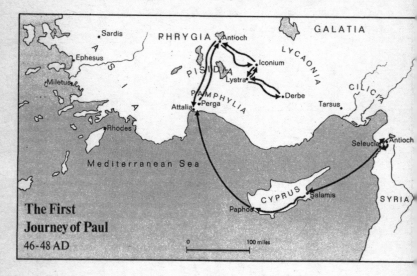

The First
Journey of Paul
46-48 AD

The Second
Journey of Paul
49-52 AD

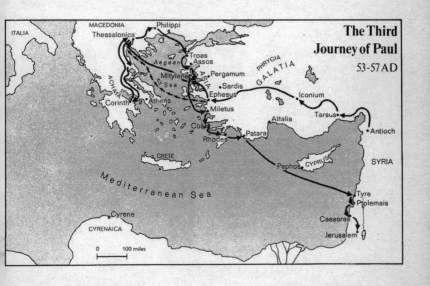

ITALIA

MACEDONIA   •Philippi

Thessalonica

Aegean

ACHAIA   Troas

Assos

Mitylene

Pergamum

PHRYGIA

GALATIA

Sea

•Sardis

Ephesus   Iconium

Corinth   Athens

Miletus   Tarsus

Attalia

Cos   Antioch

Rhodes   Patara

CRETE   Paphos   CYPRUS   SYRIA

Mediterranean Sea

Tyre
Ptolemais

Cyrene   Caesarea

CYRENAICA   Jerusalem

0   100 miles

The Third
Journey of Paul
53–57 AD

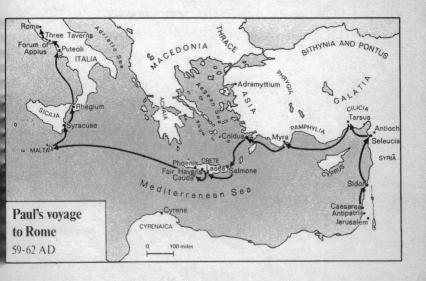

Rome•

•Three Taverns

Adriatic Sea

THRACE

BITHYNIA AND PONTUS

Forum of
Applus   •Puteoli

ITALIA   MACEDONIA

PHRYGIA

GALATIA

SICILIA   •Rhegium

ACHAIA   *Aegean*

ASIA   CILICIA

Adramyttium

Tarsus

Syracuse   PAMPHYLIA

Antioch

MALTA   Cnidus   Myra

Seleucia

SYRIA

CRETE   Salmone   CYPRUS

Phoenix

Fair Havens   Lasea

Cauda

Sidon

Mediterranean Sea

Caesarea
Antipatris

Cyrene   Jerusalem

CYRENAICA

Paul's voyage
to Rome
59–62 AD

0   100 miles

The Near East and the Aegean in the 13th Century BC

ALACA HUYUK

ZZUWATNA

CARCHEMISH

AMURRU

UGARIT

KADESH

MITANNI

NINEVEH

ASSUR

BABYLONIAN

BABYLON

TYRE

E

	Mycenaean
	Hittite
	Assyrian
	Babylonian
	Egyptian

OUTLINE HISTORY OF ASIA MINOR

EARLY TIMES

Barbarian peoples from Asia and Europe settled in Asia Minor and learned rudiments of civilisation from Mesopotamian contacts.

B.C. 3800   Brilliant neolithic civilisation (probably Hurrite) at Tel Halaf. Beginning of copper-work. Ceramics decorated with geometrical motifs. Spinning and weaving. Domestic animals but no horses.

3500   Migration from Tel Halaf across Caucasus to Mesopotamia and to Palestine.

3000   Settlements at Troy (near Dardanelles) on Anatolian plateau and Cilician plain.

2750   Troy I, trading centre for copper, gold, silver and lead. Simultaneously stone axes, catapults and maces with bone arrowheads. Troy a centre for products and techniques of metal foundries.

2500   Troy II, built by the invaders who destroyed Troy I. 'Megaron' buildings. Flourishing copper crafts replaced by bronze. Central Asia Minor dominated by Hattites, whose capital Hatti was 100 miles east of Ankara, and who appear in later Hittite archives.

HITTITES AND HURRITES

B.C. 2400 Sumerian and Akkadian conquest and export of metals to Mesopotamia.

2200 'Hieroglyphic' Hittites (as distinguished from later 'Cuneiform' Hittites) crossed the Caucasus and settled near Hatti. Virtually unknown to us – until some fifty years ago – they have become familiar through the many texts discovered at their capital Kushshar, present-day Alaca. Excavations reveal a royal burial place and skeletons in a hunched-up position, gold, silver and copper vases decorated with figures of animals, including the stag – symbol of the Hittite goddess of hunting.

2000 'Cuneiform' Hittites arrived and captured Kushshar, consolidating and developing the cities of the Cappadocian plateau. These Hittites invaded and sacked Aleppo and Babylon, within less than 100 years, becoming one of the most powerful kingdoms in all Asia Minor.

1600 Hurrites, long-time residents of Asia Minor, rose to power – but were surrounded by Sumerians, Assyrians, Egyptians and Hittites. It is probable that the Hyksos (1675–1580 B.C.) were of Hurrite origin.

The Hittite revival and Egyptian victories in Syria; the Hurrites were obliged to make matrimonial alliances, in order to survive.

1460 The Hittite empire reunified its mosaic of principalities from Cilicia to the Dardanelles, repelled an invasion from Armenia and once again invaded Syria. Palestine became the battlefield of the Egyptians and Hittites.

1200 New migrations from the west, referred to in Egyptian records as of 'The Peoples of the Sea', finally overpowered the Hittite empire.

HITTITES – LOST AND FOUND

Michael Wood, in his recent TV series and fine book, *In Search of the Trojan War*, has summarised the rediscovery of this great Bronze Age civilisation with the earliest Indo-European language, the 'Hittite branch of the tree from which Celtic, Germanic – and Greek – grew'.

Even the Classical Greeks were unaware of a Hittite empire in Asia Minor. References in the Old Testament to Hittites are frequent, but give no hint of their importance, and imply they were merely another tribe encountered by the Israelites in Palestine. There are two exceptions:

1   2 Chron. 1:17:   Solomon buys costly Egyptian horses for the Hittite kings.
2   2 Kings 7:6–7:   Israelite kings can bring the Hittites to bear against their enemies.

Such references hardly do justice to an empire stretching from the Euphrates to the Aegean!

Early archaeological evidence is sketchy and scattered. In 1812, an unknown script was discovered at Hamath (Hama) in Syria. In 1834, at Boghas Köy, a village 100 miles east of Ankara, vast fortifications a mile in perimeter were found. At one gate was a life-size figure carved in relief, with helmet, axe and short sword. Another gate was flanked by massive stone lions. At yet another was carved a procession of gods or warriors. Perimeter walls two to three miles in length equalled those of Classical Athens. A few miles to the north was a second site with a sphinx gate, still above ground. There, within an inner sanctum, protected by winged demons, was a set of twelve figures distinguished by strange hieroglyphs in an unknown language.

It was not until 1878 that British excavations at Carchemish on the Euphrates revealed another late Bronze Age palace with mud-brick walls, sculpture and hieroglyphic inscriptions that matched the ones near Ankara.

It was not until 1923 that the Oxford Professor of Assyriology linked rock carvings and hieroglyphics near Izmir, on the Aegean, with those of Carchemish on the Euphrates (746 miles to the east). He wrote: 'A powerful empire must have existed in Asia Minor possessing its own special artistic sculpture and its own special script.' And so the Hittite empire was introduced to the world.

The same Oxford professor went on to make another important equation: that the great King of Hatti who opposed and checked the warrior Pharaoh Rameses II at the famous battle of Kadesh on the Orontes in Syria was none other than the Emperor of the Hittites. The famous treaty that resulted is recorded on the temple walls at Karnak and Luxor and describes how the 'King of Hatti gathered to himself all lands as far as the ends of the sea, sixteen nations and 2,500 chariots'. These ideas were dramatically confirmed in 1887 by cuneiform tablets from the diplomatic archives of the Egyptian palace at Tell El Amarna (see Page 24). These included endless correspondence with petty kings in Syria and Palestine showing the span of the Hittite imperial alliance.

When the German archaeologists excavated the site of the imperial capital city at Boghaz Köy, east of Ankara, some 10,000 clay tablets, mainly in Hittite, but in all in eight different languages, demonstrated the multinational character of the Hittite empire. A single tablet 'enshrined' a personal letter from Rameses II to Hattusilis, the emperor, giving the exact titles and pedigrees of each ruler – exactly as in the Karnak temple text of the treaty – in beautiful cuneiform and excellent Babylonian.

The highly efficient filing system of the Hittite Foreign Office reveals a wealth of international diplomacy, including negotiations for the marriage, at her request, of the widow of Tutankhamun to a Hittite Prince Zannanza. The young prince was murdered by a rival faction of the Egyptian court, which provoked a major diplomatic crisis.

It seems unbelievable that such an empire, its capital and records should have been lost from the twelfth century B.C. to the twentieth century A.D.

Alphabet of Ugarit

UGARIT	LATIN	ARABIC	UGARIT	LATIN	ARABIC
ᗡᗡ—	A	أ	⤙	ḏ =	ذ
ᗡᗡᗡ—	B	ب	ᗡᗡᗡ—	N	ن
ᗷ	G	ج	⤙	ẓ =	ظ
ᗷ	ḫ =	خ	⤙	S	س
ᗡᗡᗡ—	D	د	ᗡ	' =	ع
ᗘ	H	ه	ᗘ	P (F)	ف
ᗷᗡᗡ—	W	و	⤙⤙	ṣ =	ص
ᗷ	Z	ز	ᗡᗷ	Q	ق
ᗡᗷᗡ	ḥ =	ح	ᗷᗡᗡ—	R	ر
ᗡᗡᗷ	ṭ =	ط	⤙	ṯ =	ث
ᗡᗡᗡ	Y	ي	⤙	ġ =	غ
ᗷᗡ—	K	ك	—ᗡ	T	ت
ᗡᗷᗷ	š =	ش	ᗘ	I	إ
ᗡᗡᗡ	L	ل	ᗘᗘᗘ	U	ؤ
ᗡᗷ	M	م	ᗘᗘᗘ	(S)	(س)

SEA PEOPLES

From 1200 B.C., the Hittite empire began to be submerged by new migrants from the west, referred to in Egyptian records as 'Peoples of the Sea', and a 'mixed multitude'. These wandered across Asia to Pamphylia (the name means 'mixed multitude').

Following the fall of Troy in 1184, Achaeans, Ionians, Aeolians and Dorians settled among the ruined Hittite cities and in their own colonies along the coastline. There were four distinct regions from west to east:

1   Lycia: the mountainous area west of Antalya; timber growing and little else.
2   Pamphylia: the coastal plain with three rivers descending to the coast, on which were five large cities: Attalia (Antalya), Perga, Sillyum, Aspendos and Side; cotton growing.
3   Rough Cilicia: Taurus Mountains reaching down to the coast in deep gorges and valleys.
4   Smooth Cilicia: a fertile cotton-growing coastal plain, on which are the cities of Mersin, Tarsus, and Adana.

There were three legendary leaders of this migration, three seers called Mopsus, Calchas and Amphilochus, between whom relations were often strained. It is doubtful whether Calchas ever reached Pamphylia, but he, together with Mopsus, is credited with the foundation of Perga. Mopsus and Amphilochus reached Cilicia, but quarrelled and killed each other in single combat.

The legendary settlement of Pamphylia by Mopsus is confirmed by independent evidence:

1   The Pamphylian dialect of Greek, both on coins at Perga and Aspendos, and on inscriptions at Sillyum, was very close to that of southern Greece *before* the Dorian invasion of Greece – *after* the fall of Troy.
2   The existence of Mopsus as a historical person and his association with Pamphylia is proved from Hittite records. On an early city site there had been found different versions of one long inscription – one version in

Phoenician and the other in Hittite hieroglyphs. In both, the king describes himself as the descendant of an ancestor named MPS in Phoenician and Muksas in Hittite. An earlier cuneiform tablet also mentions Mopsus – under the name Muksas. Mopsus was a popular name given to private individuals until the Roman empire.

7

PERSIANS AND GREEKS, ROMANS AND PIRATES

THE PERSIAN PERIL

In the year 546 B.C., the legendarily wealthy King of Lydia –
'rich as Croesus' – was defeated by the Persian Emperor
Cyrus and led into captivity at Ecbatane. The Persians
gradually occupied the coastal cities leaving garrisons to
exact tribute and to put down rebellion with great cruelty.
The great sea-bound city of Miletus revolted, but suffered
defeat in the year 494 B.C. in a naval battle off the island of
Lade.

It was after this that first Darius and, ten years later,
Xerxes set out to invade and subjugate Greece. Xerxes'
army was estimated by Herodotus at the vast figure of one
and three-quarter million men, drawn from all parts of
the empire, which stretched from the Mediterranean to
the Indus basin. The Pamphylian cities we shall visit
contributed thirty ships to the Persian fleet.

As well illustrated in the *son et lumière* on the acropolis of
Athens, the utter defeat of Darius on land at Marathon, and
of Xerxes by sea at Salamis, left Greece in control of the
Aegean. The cities of Pamphylia and Cilicia, however,
remained in the hands of their Persian garrisons, until the
Athenian general won a convincing victory by land and sea
at Aspendos. The coastal cities were briefly linked with
Athens, but within 100 years returned to Persian control.

The second period of Persian rule lasted until the coming of Alexander the Great.

THE MACEDONIAN CONQUEST

In the spring of 334 B.C., at the age of twenty, with a small but efficient army of infantry phalanxes and cavalry, Alexander crossed the Dardanelles. At Troy, he placed laurel wreaths on the legendary grave-mounds of Achilles and Patroclus. In June, Alexander met and defeated the Persians under Granicus and seized the fabulous treasure of Croesus, to help finance his campaign. After destroying the Persian fleet at Lycia, he arrived in Pamphylia, in the early spring of the following year, 333 B.C. He visited the cities of Perga, Side and Sillyum and after some resistance, he subdued Aspendos, which paid dearly for its brief bravado in extra tribute money.

That summer, Alexander reached Tarsus, where he was delayed several months by illness, before climbing up through the Cilician Gates. The following November, he defeated the Persian army under another Darius in northern Syria and gained yet a third great victory in Upper Mesopotamia. He continued on to Babylon and finally reached the Indus. He died on his return to Babylon on 13 June 323, barely ten years since he had crossed the Dardanelles.

Alexander's interest and purpose in controlling the coast we are to visit had been to deny the whole coastline as a naval base to the Persians. On his death, his empire was shared out among his quarrelling lieutenants, of whom Seleucus ruled in Asia Minor and Syria. His successors, mostly called 'Antiochus', sought to control the individual city states, but finally provoked the expedition of Roman forces into Asia. The last Antiochus was defeated by the Romans in 190 B.C., at the crucial battle of Magnesia. Some will remember the Magnesia Gate at Ephesus.

ROMANS AND PIRATES

The Romans, unwilling to burden themselves with a territory so far east, handed over power to the kings of Pergamum, the last of whom bequeathed his kingdom back to Rome in 133 B.C. The Romans gave away the outlying areas and coastline, but retained the central core of the Pergamene kingdom as the Roman province of Asia. The Romans were not concerned with the coastal cities until provoked by the activities of pirates and brigands, particularly in Cilicia.

George Bean relates how Rough Cilicia was perfect country for piracy and brigandage. Its wild and almost impenetrable character rendered the robbers safe from pursuit; the numerous tiny anchorages and occasional offshore islets afforded admirable lurking-places, and the important sea-route from Syria to the Aegean and the west led naturally along this coast. It is not surprising that piracy in these parts had been a problem since the fifth century and with the gradual weakening of the Seleucid power it had, during the course of the second century, grown to be a serious menace. The Romans at first did nothing to suppress it; on the contrary they even indirectly encouraged it, for a particular reason. Among the most profitable forms of piracy was the trade in slaves, and slaves were in enormous demand in Italy, both for the houses of the upper classes in Rome and for the farms in the country. After 167 B.C. the Romans declared the island of Delos a free port, and at once a vast slave emporium was established there; the turnover, as Strabo tells us, ran to tens of thousands in a day. But as time went on and the pirates were found to be interfering with commerce between Rome and the east, and were even venturing to harry the coasts of the province of Asia, some action became imperative. In 102 B.C. a certain Marcus Antonius, grandfather of the famous Mark Antony, was appointed with a fleet to deal with them; he succeeded in inflicting a defeat on them and seizing some of their ships. The pirates later had their revenge on him by capturing his daughter; and in general Antonius' campaign had little lasting effect.

The next Roman move was to appeal to the various friendly kings and free cities in the east to do their best to keep the seas clear for peaceful passage, but this, too – perhaps hardly surprisingly – produced little or no result. About this time also (the exact date is disputed) the Romans established a province in Cilicia, but in general the majority of governors under the republic saw in their province a source of profit for themselves.

Meanwhile the pirates flourished unchecked, and not only in Cilicia but also on the west coast of the Gulf of Antalya, where a pirate chief by the name of Zenicetes had strongly established himself as virtual ruler of the country. But not for long. In 67 B.C. Pompey was appointed to an extraordinary command with almost unlimited powers and resources for the complete and final extermination of piracy from the whole Mediterranean. His success was rapid and brilliant. Following a naval victory off Coracesium (now Alanya) he besieged the pirates in their fortresses on land, and, by granting generous terms to those who surrendered, brought his campaign to a completely satisfactory conclusion in a matter of weeks. Rough Cilicia was now added to the province, whose name thus ceased for the first time to be a misnomer, and piracy was never again so serious a nuisance to the Roman power.

Part Two:

EARLY LIFE OF SAUL

8

TARSUS

Saul, called Paul, was 'a man of Tarsus' (Acts 9:11), 'a Jew born at Tarsus in Cilicia' (Acts 22:3), 'a citizen of no mean city' (Acts 21:39).

He was essentially a Jew of the Diaspora – one of many scattered through the cities of the Roman empire for reasons of war, exile, trade or commerce. Jews of the Diaspora were 'different', speaking Greek, the lingua franca of the empire, reading the scriptures in the Greek translation, the Septuagint, influenced in their thinking and activities by their non-Jewish environment. Yet, of the same faith in the one God, they remained aloof from all pagan idolatry and immorality. Saul was a Hebrew and a Pharisee, theologically trained in Jerusalem, yet able to talk like a Greek and to quote his own native Cilician stoics before the intellectuals of Athens. He wrote, in a peculiarly 'muscular' Greek, closely argued letters and he was, by birth, a citizen of Rome. It is difficult to see how such a fusion of cultures could be found elsewhere than in Tarsus, to equip 'the apostle to the Gentiles'.

Jerome, in his *Illustrious Men*, says Saul was of the tribe of Benjamin (Rom. 11:1 and Phil. 3:5) from the town of Gischala, now El-Jish in northern Galilee, seven miles west of Hazor. Jerome says that when Gischala was captured by the Romans, Saul was taken by his parents to Tarsus, but it is far more likely that his family was well established in Tarsus long before Saul's birth. He certainly spent his youth in Tarsus and learned his trade as a tentmaker, it being the rule throughout Orthodox Jewry to train sons, whatever their social and financial prospects, to a trade.

The weavers of Tarsus still spin goats' hair to make coarse tent cloth for the nomads of Tarsus. The hair comes from herds on the Taurus Mountains, thirty miles to the north, where the snow lies until May. Consequently the goats grow long coats and their hair is famous for its great length and strength. The nomad tents are loosely woven to allow the passage of air in hot weather, but to allow the thread to swell in wet weather making the tent fabric completely waterproof. Tarsus was famed for its tough tent cloth or *cilicium*, as it was called after the province of Cilicia. The French word for hair-cloth is still *cilice*!

A Pharisee and the son of a Pharisee, destined for the rabbinate, the young Saul would have had a strict upbringing in the synagogue school. From the age of thirteen, as a 'Son of the Law', he would have joined his father in the adult worship of the synagogue at Tarsus. Then, surely, he would have attended the famous university with its magnificent facilities, the gymnasia, the theatre, the art-school and stadium – sharing all the Hellenistic culture, which his Hebrew convictions would allow. At about the age of nineteen, in the year A.D. 28 or 29, he went to Jerusalem to study under Gamaliel, a member of the sanhedrin, well known as a wise and learned 'Pharisee moderate'. Perhaps he stayed with the family of his sister (Acts 23:16).

In the year 39, following his conversion in Damascus, his retreat in Arabia and his return to Damascus, he visited Jerusalem (Acts 9:30), but was immediately sent home to Tarsus by the 'brethren'. Some five years later, Barnabas collected Saul and took him back to Antioch, where they both taught together for a whole year. Just what Saul did in that time at Tarsus is not told, but Saul is hardly likely not to have preached Christ up and down Cilicia. There are a number of punishments unaccounted for in his list of sufferings in 2 Corinthians 11 and this was probably a very uncomfortable five years of his ministry, without any apostolic support. On both his second and third missionary journeys, Saul – now Paul – must have passed through Tarsus on his way out from Antioch. The second journey took him 'through Syria and Cilicia' (Acts 15:41), and third journey 'through Galatia and Phrygia' (Acts 18:23).

Tarsus, in the centre of the Cilician plain below the Taurus Mountains, was at a strategic crossroads. Originally sited well inland as a precaution against pirates, the plague of the Cilician coastline, the ancient city of Tarsus was bisected by the River Cydnus which flowed out into the Lake of Rhegma, five miles further towards the sea. A skilfully engineered harbour on the lakeside could accommodate sizeable ships, and small craft – like Cleopatra's barge – could reach the city centre up the Cydnus. For it was here that the Egyptian queen first 'pursed up' Antony's heart, as Shakespeare put it. The historian Plutarch described the golden stern, the purple sails, the silver oars, the music of flutes, pipes and harps. Perhaps Paul's father had actually witnessed the scene. Certainly, Paul will have listened to old men who remembered it.

Owing to flood damage to both city and harbour, Justinian diverted the river channel east of the city and allowed only minor streams to flow through the centre. Today, one can look north up the river valley and beyond to the foothills of the Taurus range. William Ramsey describes Tarsus as 'a city with its feet resting on a great inland harbour and its head reaching up to the hills'.

Little is known of the early history of Tarsus. Archaeology has revealed Neolithic stone tools and pottery from 5000 B.C. and a succession of Bronze Age cities from 3000 to 1200. The city was captured by the Assyrian Shalmanezer III in the mid ninth century and destroyed by Senacherib in 696 B.C. It was occupied by the Persians, who ruled Tarsus through a puppet-king. Cyrus led an army of 10,000 Greek mercenaries through the city. Alexander the Great arrived in 333 B.C. and on his death, Tarsus became part of the Syrian empire ruled from Antioch. Under the Seleucids, the city was renamed 'Antioch on the Cydnus', but Syrian ambitions westward clashed with Roman interests, and Cilicia became a borderland. In 65 B.C., the Roman occupation was completed by Pompey, and Cilicia became a Roman province with Tarsus as its capital, with a population of half a million.

Pompey probably found the Tarsian Jews a useful force for law and order – concerned as they were with commerce and finance – and he rewarded them accordingly, some by Roman citizenship. Their Roman privilege passed by right of birth to Paul and others. Cicero became governor of Tarsus in 50 or 51 B.C. and set out to subdue the bandit-ridden hinterland. Mark Antony welcomed Cleopatra here in 38 B.C. The historian Strabo (63 B.C.–A.D. 21) wrote: 'The people of Tarsus have devoted themselves so eagerly, not only to philosophy, but also to the whole round of education in general – that they have surpassed Athens, Alexandria and other schools of philosophy.'

Tarsus indeed was renowned as a centre of Stoic philosophy of which the founder was Zeno of Kition in the fourth century. The 'second founder' in the third century was Chrysippus, born at Soli near Tarsus. In the same century the poet Aratus (whom Paul quoted on Mars Hill) was also born at Soli. So, Stoicism was a strong influence in the intellectual life of Tarsus. The Tarsian Athenadorus became tutor to the young Augustus in Rome. When he returned he became governor of the city. His final advice to Augustus was, 'When you are angry, Caesar, say nothing and do nothing until you have repeated to yourself the letters of the alphabet.'

Admittedly, some of Paul's letters were written 'red-hot' to deal with specific emergencies, but many of his Epistles reflect a very studied and controlled philosophy. And the sheer courage with which he faced recurring opposition and physical punishment reflect a massive stoicism. 'I have learnt to be content, to manage with whatever I have. I know how to be poor and I know how to be rich too. I have been through my initiation and now I am ready for anything anywhere' (Phil. 4:11 ff.).

The first Christian churches in Tarsus were probably built in the fourth century. There was a church of St Peter outside the city and a church of St Paul within the city by the sixth century. The Crusaders captured Tarsus in the eleventh century, and the Ottoman Turks in the sixteenth century.

It takes a great deal of imagination to conjure up the river and harbour, the baths and statues, the agora and theatre of Paul's time in the Tarsus of today. The Roman/Hellenistic city is buried far below the present town. Of its three gates, the Valley, the Mountain and the Sea Gates, perhaps the last is marked by a monumental arch at the approach to the town from Mersin. This rather questionable Roman/Byzantine construction is variously called 'St Paul's Gate', 'Cleopatra's Gate' and 'the Gate of the Bitch'. Not much further into the town on the left is a deep well which tradition associates with the boy Saul. Visitors can still buy the coarse dark goat-hair weaves from the Taurus, within the *suq*.

Despite the almost total lack of archaeological evidence, the town is full of old houses, gardens and waterfalls of considerable charm. They still preserve the aura of an ancient and strategic city built at a crossroads in history, but now buried some twenty feet below the Cilician silt.

Scripture References:
Acts   9:11 and 30
         11:25 and 26
         21:37–22:3

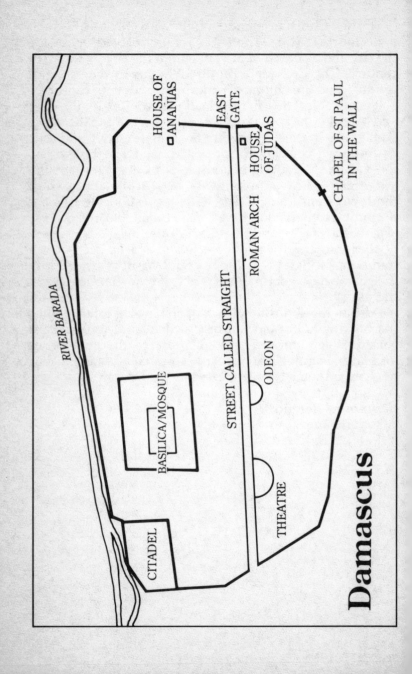

Damascus

RIVER BARADA

CITADEL

BASILICA/MOSQUE

THEATRE

ODEON

STREET CALLED STRAIGHT

ROMAN ARCH

HOUSE OF JUDAS

EAST GATE

HOUSE OF ANANIAS

CHAPEL OF ST PAUL IN THE WALL

9

DAMASCUS

The oasis of Damascus is at the crossroads of the Nile and Euphrates river civilisations, on an ancient caravan route following the Fertile Crescent.

Saul the Pharisee almost certainly travelled the spine of Judea from Jerusalem, probably skirting the sites of Shechem, Samaria and Dothan, to join the Via Maris below Nazareth, on the Plain of Esdraelon. From there he would possibly pass Nain, to reach the Lake of Galilee at Magdala. Then, following the road round the lake to Capernaum, he crossed the Jordan Delta into the territory of Herod Philip. Climbing up on to the Golan, he would pass Caesarea Philippi on the slopes of Mount Hermon and so reach the Gardens of Damascus.

It is perhaps less likely that he followed the less hospitable desert route over Trachonitis. This turned east at Shechem, through Bethshan and the Decapolis, to cut across the dry volcanic uplands of Trachonitis. This route meant negotiating a long, lonely stretch of desert, vulnerable to raiding parties and brigands. By either route, the journey would be a good six days' travel over 150 miles.

The fanatical young Pharisee was hounding down a new minority in the synagogues of Damascus, under warrant from the high priest in Jerusalem. The latter had no real authority over Jews in the Syrian capital, but the Romans had placed the city under the rule of the King of Petra, Aretas IV. Maybe the Nabatean ruler connived at such a project and enabled Saul's inquisitorial intervention and even his deportation of suspects. The whole scheme smacked of the arrogance of the Jerusalem high priesthood.

In the first century, both Jews and Greeks infiltrated the cities of the civilised world. In Damascus, the Jewish colony was very powerful. Josephus recorded that 18,000 Jews were massacred there, during the Jewish Revolt of A.D. 66–70.

Thirty years previously, the Greek-speaking element in the Jewish-Christian community had provoked considerable persecution from the Jewish high priest. Stephen's indictment of the authorities for their reliance upon the Temple and his scriptural arguments for the messiahship of Jesus had particularly incensed the young Saul. Thus, he set out with a fanatical determination to defend the honour of God and to destroy this heresy, commissioned by the high priest to arrest any followers of 'the Way' he could find.

Riding out of the North, or Damascus, Gate of Jerusalem, he would pass the place of execution, where he had been an accessory to the stoning of Stephen. Over the spine of Judea and Samaria, in the saddle by day, under the stars by night, he had plenty of time to think. Out into the Plain of Esdraelon, he was faced with Nazareth on the northern skyline, the home of the 'accursed Carpenter', founder of the Way – who called himself 'The Way, the Truth and the Life'.

Turning towards the lake, the road took him round through Magdala, Bethsaida and Capernaum, home of the Carpenter's crew. Capernaum had been the headquarters of that heretical movement, whose members claimed their Messiah had risen from the dead and was still alive.

As the cavalcade emerged from the desert soil to reach the verge of the *ghuta* or gardens, at about noon on the sixth day out, their leader was suddenly blinded by a shaft of light and fell to the ground. There, he heard a voice penetrating the darkness: 'Saul, Saul, why do you persecute me? I am Jesus, whom you are persecuting. Rise and enter the city and you will be told what you are to do.' So,

the living Carpenter stopped him in his tracks and spoke
face to face.

Some six miles south-west of the city is the Kaukab Hill,
on the very edge of the Golan Desert, from which the
emerald green of the oasis extends into the distance to the
city centre, circled by the cliffs and foothills of the Anti-
Lebanon. Today, a disused Orthodox church claims the site
of the Conversion. Michelangelo's painting on the ceiling of
the Sistine Chapel shows Jesus reaching down his hand
towards a Saul fallen to the ground and covering his
sightless eyes.

Saul's companions led him blind and helpless into the
city, where he fasted for three days. Then in a vision, a
Christian disciple called Ananias was told to visit him in the
house of Judas, in Straight Street. He was to welcome him
and baptise him, and then to unfold the divine commission
of this 'apostle to the Gentiles'.

Both before the sanhedrin in Jerusalem and before Herod
Agrippa at Caesarea, Saul clearly recalled the words of
Ananias, the timid fugitive to the Grand Inquisitor himself:
'Brother Saul . . . The God of our fathers has appointed you
to know his will, to see the Just One [the Living Carpenter]
and to hear from his own mouth, you will be a witness for
him to all men of what you have seen and heard' (Acts
22:13–15).

The 'Street called Straight' is still the east-west axis of the
city, its central *suq* and market street. Once it was
colonnaded like all great Greco-Roman streets, now it is
roofed in places with corrugated iron! Walls still surround
the Roman city, and the level of the Roman East Gate, still
standing, shows the level of the city in the time of Saul.

Medieval Christian traditions focus on a 'house of
Ananias', north of the main street and a church of St Paul
set within a medieval gate in the picturesque east wall of the
city.

The next few days and weeks following his 'Conversion'
were to witness a pattern of events which, so often
repeated, led to a final severance between Church and

Synagogue and to the Gentile ministry of St Paul. All the familiar elements were present in a sequence of events that followed Paul, wherever he went: preaching in the Synagogue, which achieved a bridgehead for evangelism which inevitably led to dispute and opposition.

In Damascus, the trained mind from Tarsus, schooled by Gamaliel, was more than a match for the local rabbis. They appealed to the civil authorities – as did Caiaphas and so many more in years to come. With the exception of Gallio at Corinth, the authorities were persuaded. In this situation Saul escaped over the wall without dignity and expressed his annoyance in a letter to Corinth: 'I had to be let down over the wall in a hamper, through a window.'

With the tension in Damascus relieved, the Nabatean King Aretas would not be likely to notice a quiet refugee busy with his books and prayers, in some quiet corner of his kingdom. After all, Damascus was the north-west gate of Arabia. Saul withdrew from, and returned through, Damascus, a changed man charged with his mission to the Gentiles, and returned to Tarsus, whence he was collected by Barnabas.

From the earliest occupation of the Near East, man has congregated on the edge of fertility and on the shore of the much-travelled desert. Damascus is indispensable, to the urbanised and to the nomad alike. Watered by Naaman's 'Rivers of Damascus', the Garden City has outlived Antioch, Nineveh and Babylon and was for 100 years the world capital of the Ummayyads.

Today, Damascus is one of the most stable capital cities of the Near East, whose president has been in power nearly twenty years.

Scripture References:
2 Kings 5:1–14
Isaiah 7:8; 8:3 and 4; 17:1–3
Amos 1:3–5
Acts   9:1–30
       22:6–16
       26:12–20

10

ANTIOCH ON THE ORONTES

APPROACH AND LOCALITY

From Tarsus we travel some 250 kilometres (156 miles) round, under the armpit of Asia and enter the region of the Hatay, which extends down to the frontier. From the turn south, the road descends through a gorge into the Plain of Issus, famous as the site of the decisive defeat of the Persians under Darius III by Alexander the Great in 333 B.C.

Somewhat delayed by the illness which nearly killed him at Tarsus, Alexander the Great reached the Plain of Issus in early November. Either in ignorance of the Macedonian conqueror's advance, or in an attempt to cut him off from his bases, the Persian troops suddenly pounced on the rearguard of the Macedonians. The Macedonians thus turned back, although they had already reached Myriandus, at the end of the Gulf of Iskenderun. At the start of the battle, Alexander was thus separated from his bases by the Persian army. Darius III gathered the greater part of his cavalry commanded by General Nabarsanes on his right, put his Greek mercenaries in the centre and his light infantry on the right flank. Alexander opposed his Thessalian cavalry to the troops of Nabarsanes, set his heavy Macedonian phalanx in the centre and a corps of archers reinforced with 300 horsemen of the élite from his own personal guard on the right flank, against the Persian infantry (which was scattered from the very beginning).

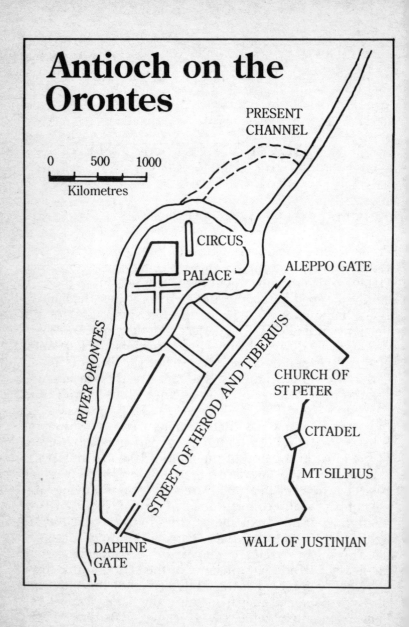

Antioch on the Orontes

PRESENT
CHANNEL

0   500   1000

Kilometres

CIRCUS

PALACE

ALEPPO GATE

RIVER ORONTES

STREET OF HEROD AND TIBERIUS

CHURCH OF
ST PETER

CITADEL

MT SILPIUS

DAPHNE
GATE

WALL OF JUSTINIAN

The very first charge upset the lines of the Persians, while the powerful phalanx crossed the little river, separating the two armies, to come to grips with the Greek mercenaries. Alexander, with part of the cavalry, came to the help of the phalanx when it got into difficulties. On seeing the royal chariot, Alexander made his way through the Persian lines and a terrible mêlée began around the chariot of Darius, who fled on horseback. His troops dispersed when they realised the king had abandoned them and Nabarsanes retreated into Cilicia. The retreat was so sudden that the imperial family and the king's baggage were not evacuated in time and fell into the hands of the Macedonians. The victory opened up the way for Alexander into Syria, which was later conquered by the Macedonians.

Beyond Dort Yol, we follow the coast road to Iskenderun, better known as Alexandretta, past a huge sixteenth-century caravanserai at Yakacik, whose architect was the great Sinan, who built the Suleimaniye Mosque in Istanbul. Iskenderun is a busy port – a fusion of Mediterranean, Anatolian and Syrian cultures. Thence, the road winds steeply through the pass up to Belem with spectacular views. We may have time to divert to the Mamluk castle at Bagras, as we descend to Lake Amik and the Orontes Valley, before we reach Antioch.

The city lies between Mount Silpius, nearly 2,000 feet high, and the Orontes, which rises in the Beqa'a Valley between the Lebanon ranges. There were no fewer than sixteen Antiochs, all established by Seleucus Nicator (312–281 B.C.), founder of the Seleucid dynasty who had been one of Alexander's generals. The name 'Antioch' was that of Seleucus' father, his son and his successor Antiochus Soter. Antioch on the Orontes was the ideal headquarters of an empire which included Asia Minor, the Euphrates Valley and Persia. It was at the centre of the Fertile Crescent, on a caravan route from the Euphrates to the Mediterranean, almost opposite the island of Cyprus and only 300 miles north of Jerusalem. A road ran from the city south-west to the port of Seleucia, now called Samandag (Acts 13:4). The harbour is almost completely silted up and only a small port remains.

HISTORY

From its foundation, the town had many fine monuments, temples and public buildings. It grew fast into a lively and tumultuous city with a very mixed population: Macedonian and Cretan settlers speaking Greek, local inhabitants speaking Aramaic and a large community of Jews speaking Hebrew. By the second century B.C., there were half a million inhabitants in what had become both a great business centre and a city of great luxury, famous for its splendid games and feasts in honour of Apollo.

At the end of the Seleucid dynasty, the Syrians – fed up with Seleucid family squabbles – invited the King of Armenia, Tigranes the Great, to Antioch, which he occupied in 83 B.C. The city enjoyed fourteen years' peace, before the arrival of the Romans in 64 B.C. Pompey invaded Syria and declared it a Roman province, but left Antioch and Seleucia as free cities. Mark Antony and Cleopatra were married in 40 B.C. at the Sanctuary of Apollo at Daphne – a southern suburb of Antioch. Augustus visited the city in both 30 and 20 B.C. Herod the Great paved the main street in marble.

Despite frequent earthquakes, particularly in A.D. 37 and 115 when the visiting Emperor Trajan was nearly killed, Antioch remained an important trading centre and became a centre of arts and sciences, theology and philosophy. The famous Cilician poet, Aratus, spent several years at the Seleucid court and it was from his 'Phenomena' that Paul quoted on Mars Hill: 'We are all his children', meaning that as God's children the Athenians were illogical in worshipping man-made images (Acts 17:28, 29). Antioch was destined to become the earliest missionary headquarters of the Christian Church.

CHRISTIANITY

Because of the dispersion of Hellenised Christians after the stoning of Stephen, the Gentile Christian community scattered through the Levant. Whether through Christians from Cyprus or Jerusalem, the Church was firmly established in Antioch. The Church there and Barnabas, in turn, chose Paul as his assistant, collecting him from Tarsus, some eighty sea miles across the Gulf of Iskenderun, or Hatay. It was about this time, A.D. 46, that the possibly derisive title of 'Christians' was first given to members of the Church of Antioch.

In all this success Barnabas did not forget his old friends of Jerusalem. There, the stewardship experiment was breaking down under the strain of poor crops and other difficulties. The Antiochene Christians had started a Judean relief fund. Barnabas and Paul were chosen for the happy task of delivering their contributions to Jerusalem, whence they returned to Antioch, bringing with them Barnabas' young nephew, John Mark. The spontaneous success of the young Church in Antioch promoted new enterprise and it was natural that the same team should be sent off on the first missionary journey of 1,400 miles in the year A.D. 45 or 46 (Acts 13:1–3).

On their return, they reported at length on their progress, particularly on 'how God had opened the door of faith to the pagans'. Consequently, when representatives of the Jerusalem Church arrived with demands that the Gentile Christians be circumcised, it was Paul and Barnabas who were sent to plead the case of the Antiochene Christians in Jerusalem. At what has become known as 'The First Council' (Acts 15), it was Peter who insisted on Paul and Barnabas receiving a full hearing for their Galatian report; thereafter James – as chairman – gave a verdict generous to the Gentiles. This was conveyed by delegates from Jerusalem, accompanying Paul and Barnabas back to Antioch. The men chosen were Judas Barsabbas, and Silas, who was to become Paul's companion on the next journey.

The Christian community at Antioch was delighted to receive both the deputation and their message from the council. When Paul and Barnabas discussed their next venture, they disagreed on the taking of young John Mark, who had deserted them in Pamphylia on their first journey – Paul rejecting him and Barnabas wanting to take him. As a result the two divided, Barnabas taking Mark back to Cyprus and Paul selecting Silas, another Roman citizen, to return to Galatia overland in the year 50. These two extended their journey into Europe and, two and a half years later, returned to Antioch again, landing at Caesarea and presumably travelling up the coast to Antioch.

Here, he spent a short time before continuing his journey through the Galatian country and then through Phrygia. The third missionary journey had begun and Paul was destined not to return to Ephesus, but to Jerusalem. We do not know if his journey to Rome, under escort, included a landing at Antioch, between Tyre and Myra – probably not.

The Antiochene suburb of Daphne – an area of waterfalls, oaks, cypress and laurels – was the place where in mythology Apollo pursued the nymph Daphne, who tried to escape him by changing into a laurel tree. Many temples were built in this beautiful spot three miles south of the city – to Apollo, Aphrodite, Artemis, Isis and Zeus. Here, too, a stadium was provided for games instituted by Claudius as Olympic Games, in rivalry to Greece. Titus went to Antioch after the fall of Jerusalem and built a theatre, in the process destroying a Jewish synagogue and placing a statue of Vespasian there, marked with the inscription 'from the spoils of Judea'. Josephus described Antioch as the third city in the empire, after Rome and Alexandria, and said that the Greek community was interested in Judaism, including presumably 'Nicholas of Antioch, a convert to Judaism' (Acts 6:5).

There is no doubt that St Peter went to Antioch, before Paul wrote to the Galatians (2:11). Paul opposed Peter's conduct towards Gentiles, on the grounds that his policy suggested that the only true Christians were converted

Above: The city wall, near the East Gate today

Left: Within the gate: relief of Paul's escape in a basket

Below: St Paul's Gate in the South East Wall

TARSUS AND ANTIOCH

Above: Orthodox church in Tarsus today

Below: Tarsus mosaic in museum at Antioch

Left: Rock-hewn church of St Peter at Antioch

Right: Tarsus-type goat hair tent

PISIDIAN ANTIOCH

et above: Hadrian's arch in the East Wall of
alia

Above: Aqueduct entering West Gate of
Antioch

tant view overlooking site of city

PERGAMUM

Acropolis showing Theatre, Trajaneum and Library

Sacred Way looking back from Asklepeion to Acropolis

Above: Place of Lydia's baptism in the River Gangites

Left: Via Egnatia between Neapolis and Philippi

Below: Paul's prison between Forum and Acropolis

Inset below: Relief of sacrificial bull on theatre stage

THESSALONICA

Lion memorial to
Philip of Macedon a
Amphipolis

Acropolis walls looking down on the city today

Arch of Galerius: shows him offering sacrifice at a triumph

opagus (Mars Hill) from the Acropolis

l's approach through Agora as seen from Areopagus

CORINTH

Above: Agora of ancient Corinth. Acro-Corinth in background

Left: Road from Agora to Port of Lechaeum, on the Gulf

Left: Port of Cenchreae today, the Aegean Sea

Jews who observed the Law. This threatened to produce two separate communities that could not even meet for Eucharist. Peter's behaviour should have expressed his real attitude, but instead he disguised it (Gal. 2:13).

According to local tradition, Peter preached and baptised, and the local Christians took refuge in the Grotto or Church of St Peter, a natural cavern in the rocky side of Mount Staurin, within the city walls, a quarter of a mile from the theatre. Within the grotto church fragments of early Byzantine mosaic remain, but the exterior façade is Crusader and recently restored. In the thirteenth century the grotto came into the hands of the Armenians, who left a fresco on the upper back wall with the name of Peter, 'Bedros'. It was later in Orthodox hands and is now in the hands of the Capuchins, who seek to prove the association with Peter.

Other Christian traditions include a cave, pointed out by John Chrysostom on the slope of Mount Silpius, where Paul was reputed to have lived and taught. Paul and Barnabas were said to have preached in a street near the pantheon, rebuilt by Julius Caesar – but no exact area is known.

According to the *Recognitions of Clement* (a third-century work), while Peter was in Antioch, a prominent citizen named Theophilus gave his huge house for a church, together with a special chair for St Peter. Later Theodoret mentions a 'throne' of St Peter in the possession of the city of Antioch. He takes the precedence of Antioch over Alexandria (Peter's over Mark's see) on the relative importance of the prince – apostle over the evangelist.

There were many churches in Antioch: the 'old' church in the ancient port of Antioch, probably destroyed by Diocletian and soon restored in the early fourteenth century.

The 'new' church, built by Constantine and completed by his son Constantius, was dedicated in 341 in the presence of ninety bishops, who remained for an Ecumenical Council. Eusebius describes the church as unparalleled in size and beauty. It was known also as the 'Great' or 'Golden' church, an octagon in a vast courtyard – a possible prototype for the fifth-century Church of St Simeon Stylites. Destroyed and rebuilt several times, by conquest and earthquake, no trace now survives.

Scripture References:
Acts 12:24–13:3
      15:1–3; 30–40

Part Three:

FIRST MISSIONARY JOURNEY

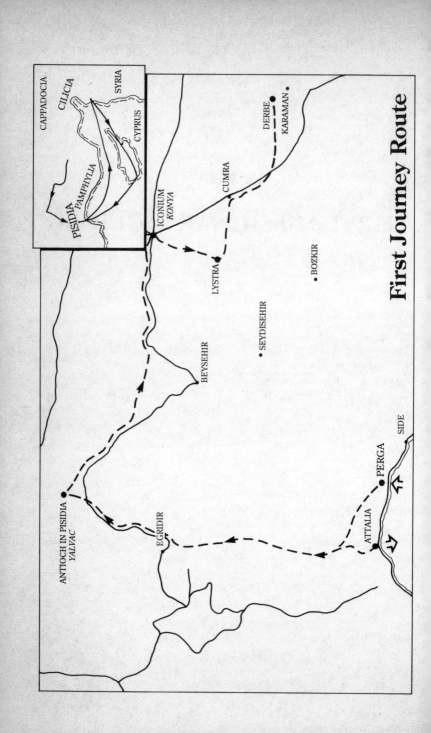

First Journey Route

11

CYPRUS

At the very outset of Paul's first missionary journey, he and Barnabas, with John Mark to assist them, sailed from Seleucia to Cyprus, landed at Salamis and went through the whole island as far as Paphos (Acts 13:4–6).

The island of Cyprus is at the crossroads of the eastern Mediterranean, a meeting place of the sea-routes from Syria, Asia Minor and Egypt on to the west. The distance of Asia Minor to the north is fifty miles, of Syria to the east seventy miles, of Egypt to the south 240 miles. The main part of the island is ninety miles east to west and no more than fifty miles north to south. In addition there is the long panhandle peninsula, which Ptolemy calls the 'Ox Tail'. Compared to other Mediterranean islands, Cyprus is larger than Crete and Corsica, and smaller than Sicily and Sardinia.

There are two ranges of mountains, the northern range called Kyrenia, which rises over 3,000 feet and the western range called Troodos, rising to nearly 6,500 feet. Two rivers run through the central plain to reach the sea at Salamis on the east coast. The climate is much like that of Palestine, with harvest in the spring and a long, hot, dry summer.

In raw materials, Cyprus is rich in copper. References to the export of copper are found in texts from Ebla (2400 B.C.), Mari (1800 B.C.) and Amarna (1400 B.C.). In fact, the Greek name for the island and for copper are the same: *kupros*. Even today more than a million tons of raw copper are

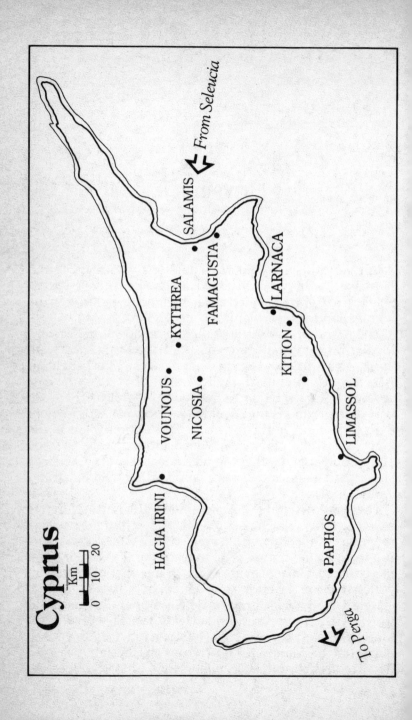

being extracted from a single mine each year, from veins that were being mined 3,000 years ago!

The Old Testament name, 'Kittim', is a Hebrew term for 'islands' in Ezekiel 27:6, Daniel 11:30, 1 Maccabees 1:1, Isaiah 23:1 and the Dead Sea Scrolls.

Archaeological excavations continue. Stone Age settlements have been found in the south, near Limassol. Bronze Age trade with Syria, Palestine and Egypt has left Cypriot pottery in Lachish and Amarna. By 1200 B.C. Greeks began to settle on the island, at Salamis, Paphos and elsewhere, leaving much Mycenaean pottery. The Iron Age, 1000 B.C., marked the arrival of Phoenicians, establishing colonies particularly at Kition, near Larnaca in the south-east. Hiram, King of Tyre and friend of Solomon, had governors on the island.

Later, both Assyrians and Persians occupied Cyprus, which supported Alexander at the battle at Issus and thereafter became part of the Hellenistic world under the Ptolemies of Egypt, who called themselves Kings of Egypt and Cyprus. The governor of Cyprus – who was at once general, admiral and high priest – resided first at Salamis and later at Paphos, supplying metal and timber for shipbuilding.

In 58 B.C., Cyprus was annexed by Rome and in 52 Cicero became governor. In 22 B.C., Cyprus became a senatorial province, so that on the arrival of Barnabas and Paul, there was a proconsul resident at Paphos.

In later history, Cyprus was fought over by Byzantines, Muslims and Crusaders – passing from Richard Coeur de Lion to the Templars to Guy de Lusignan, whose family ruled the island until 1475. During the Venetian occupation, vast fortifications and castles were built. During the Turkish occupation, there were frequent revolts and heavy taxation from 1571. The British received Cyprus (in preference to St Anne's Church, Jerusalem) as a reward for their part in the Crimean War! The Republic of Cyprus was established under Archbishop Makarios in 1960.

In Greek mythology, Cyprus is the island of Aphrodite

(Roman Venus), 'fair, golden and beautiful', from the sea-foam somewhere between Limassol and Paphos. In Greek philosophy, at the Phoenician colony of Kition, Zeno, the founder of Stoicism, was born. From Ptolemaic times, many Jews settled in Cyprus. Barnabas, a Levite by tribe, was a Hellenistic Jew, a native of the island with considerable estates there, which probably accounts for his choice of Cyprus as the first missionary target of the Church at Antioch.

SALAMIS

Paul and Barnabas arrived at Salamis from Seleucia. The port was five miles north of Famagusta, in the curve of Famagusta Bay, with a well-protected harbour. Salamis at that time was a main port and principal city, on several occasions destroyed by earthquake, rebuilt by Romans and finally destroyed by the Arab invasion of 647, when the Christian population moved to Famagusta. There, the harbour citadel of the medieval city is the supposed scene of Shakespeare's *Othello*.

At Salamis, the surviving ruins are mostly late Roman and Byzantine. They include a first-century B.C. theatre for 15,000 spectators, a gymnasium and agora, and both the Basilica of St Epiphanius, Bishop of Salamis in 357 and particularly the restored fifth-century Monastery of St Barnabas.

From Salamis, Paul and Barnabas 'travelled the whole length of the island' to Paphos. Acts 13:6 may be translated, 'made a missionary progress through the whole island'. They could have taken an inland route up the Pedieos River past Nicosia, skirting the Troodos range down to Limassol and so along the coast to Paphos, or they could have followed the coast, visiting the coastal cities, all the way. They probably took the coastal route in order to visit the ancient city of Kition.

PAPHOS

We are unable to cross nowadays from Northern Cyprus over to Paphos, the capital city of the island until the fourth century. When Paul and Barnabas reached Paphos, the Roman proconsul was Sergius Paulus. A certain magus, a Jewish false prophet named Bar-Jesus, was associated with the proconsul.

Here Paul, as a Roman citizen himself, stepped forward as spokesman to confront the false prophet. Earlier in Acts, he had been a Jew among Jews, called by his Jewish name 'Saul'. Now, before the Roman official, as himself a Roman citizen, Paul is referred to by Luke as 'Saul, who is also called Paul' (Acts 13:9), and from then on only as 'Paul'.

When Paul went on his second missionary journey, Barnabas and his young nephew Mark returned to Cyprus (Acts 15:39). The apocryphal Acts of Barnabas (fifth century?) consecrated a certain Heracleides – who had known Paul at Kition – as bishop of the island. During a further confrontation with the magus Bar-Jesus, Barnabas was burned to death in the hippodrome and Mark escaped to Alexandria.

In 478, the then Bishop of Cyprus discovered the tomb of Barnabas and the Monastery of St Barnabas was founded near Salamis. By virtue of its link with Barnabas, the Orthodox Church of Cyprus claims to be an independent branch of the Orthodox Church and elects its own archbishop.

Scripture References:
Acts 13:4–13
    15:36–39

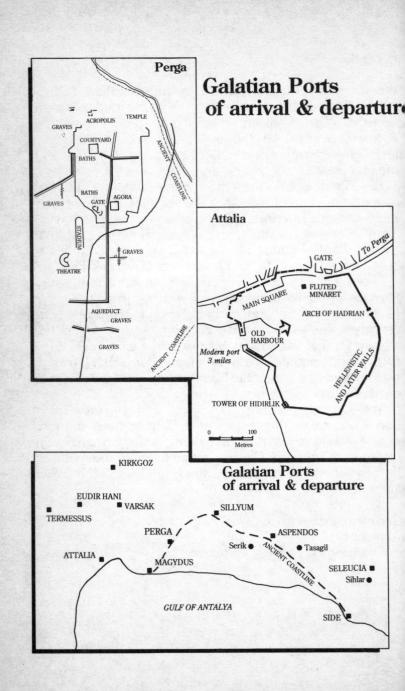

Perga

GRAVES
ACROPOLIS TEMPLE
COURTYARD
BATHS
BATHS
GRAVES GATE AGORA
STADIUM
THEATRE
GRAVES
AQUEDUCT GRAVES
GRAVES
ANCIENT COASTLINE
ANCIENT COASTLINE

Galatian Ports
of arrival & departure

Attalia

To Perga
GATE
FLUTED MINARET
MAIN SQUARE
ARCH OF HADRIAN
OLD HARBOUR
Modern port 3 miles
HELLENISTIC AND LATER WALLS
TOWER OF HIDIRLIK

0   100
Metres

Galatian Ports
of arrival & departure

KIRKGOZ
EUDIR HANI VARSAK
TERMESSUS
SILLYUM
PERGA ASPENDOS
Serik ● ● Tasagil
ATTALIA
MAGYDUS ANCIENT COASTLINE
SELEUCIA ■
Sihlar ●
GULF OF ANTALYA
SIDE

12

PERGA AND ATTALIA: PORTS OF GALATIA

FROM CYPRUS

Paul, Barnabas and John Mark landed from Paphos at either Perga or Attalia, on the Pamphylian coast. Luke only mentions *Perga* at this point: 'from Paphos to Perga' (Acts 13:13), but makes Paul return to Perga and actually sail from *Attalia* for Antioch in Syria.

TO GALATIA

The Roman province of Galatia included the whole of the centre of what we know as Asia Minor and was divided into a number of 'regions'.

'To the Churches of Galatia', Paul wrote in Galatians 1:2 and he probably had in mind all those cities and the Roman province of Galatia. Latin and Greek were the languages of the government and literature, but the mass of the people spoke their own languages and worshipped their own gods. Their Asiatic deities became identified with those of Greece and Rome and were called by Greek and Roman names, but retained their primitive characters (Acts 14:11, 12). With the advent of Christianity, these ancient religions expressed themselves in emotional movements, branded as heresies by the Orthodox Church.

ATTALIA – Acts 14:25

Attalia was the main port of entry for travellers from Syria and Egypt. The city lies on a flat limestone shelf, 120 feet above the seashore, with steep cliffs.

From the harbour, Venetian steps lead up into the town; St Paul must have climbed up, through another passage cut in the rock. The town walls run round the city from either side of the harbour. On the south side of the harbour is the Tower of Hidirlik, built in the second century A.D. and probably used as a lighthouse. On the east of the city, the Gate of Hadrian (A.D. 130) has three arches and carved decoration. On the south is the Kesik, a truncated minaret, on the site of a Roman temple, later a Byzantine church and under the Seljuks a mosque. On the north is a thirteenth-century fluted minaret. A new museum out on the road to Lycia holds remains from Perga. The view of mountains along the west coast and inland is staggering from this point.

PERGA – Acts 13:13, 14

The River Kestros flowed out into the Mediterranean only five miles east of the Roman city of Perga. Perhaps Paul sailed up the river to a port nearer the city. Strabo describes: 'Sailing up the Kestros River, one comes to Perga the city.' Perga was believed by its inhabitants to have been founded by Greek heroes from the Trojan War. Mopsos and Calchas are mentioned as the founders in inscriptions on statue bases.

In 333 B.C., Alexander passed through the city twice. From the second century B.C., there are coins of Perga depicting the cult statue of Artemis Pergaia standing within a temple. This temple was plundered of its treasures by a Roman governor in 79 B.C., but otherwise the city prospered under the Romans until the fourth century A.D.

Since 1967, Perga has been excavated by Turkish

archaeologists. There is a fine Greco-Roman theatre with seats for 15,000 spectators. The second-century stage building stands two tiers high, richly decorated with reliefs of mythological scenes featuring Dionysus and the local river-god Kestros. In the late Roman period, the theatre was used for gladiatorial shows and beast fights, with an extra parapet built upon the lower seats to protect the audience.

A second-century stadium, the best preserved after Aphrodisias, accommodated 12,000. Just outside the city gate was the tomb of the rich benefactress, Plancia Magna. The first entrance gate is Roman, the second Hellenistic, with a large horseshoe-shaped courtyard, flanked by two large round towers. The Hellenistic walls were faced with marble, with niches for statues, and are still well preserved on the east and west sides. The walls on the south side are fourth-century Roman.

Within the gate, the city street runs due north, the baths on the west side and an agora on the east. On the far, north-west, side of the main crossroads is a gymnasium (literally *palaestra* – for wrestling) dedicated to the Emperor Claudius (A.D. 41–54). Beyond this, outside the city walls is a street of tombs.

The acropolis was on a low hill north of the city, but the only ruins found there were Byzantine. There were two Byzantine churches also within the city, and one on a hill to the south-east. The famous Temple of Artemis has not been located, but inscriptions show that Aphrodite, Apollo, Hermes, Hercules and other Greek gods were worshipped here.

St Paul would have walked within these Hellenistic walls, would have seen the theatre and gymnasium, dedicated to the reigning emperor. Perga is an impressive site, second or third only to Ephesus, and perhaps Miletus, within Asia Minor.

The only fact we know from Acts about Paul in Perga is that here John Mark left the party and returned to Jerusalem. We may never know for certain *why*, but, as Barnabas later took his young nephew back to Cyprus, we might guess that Mark's withdrawal concerned the relationship, and perhaps a policy disagreement, between his Uncle Barnabas and the apostle Paul. In Cyprus, Barnabas on his own home ground had been the natural leader. At Paphos in the Roman world, Paul as Roman citizen had taken the initiative. Perhaps young Mark had resented the change in leadership, and the decision to turn from the coast inland through the dangerous mountains to Roman Galatia. Perhaps, again, the party went down with malaria in that flat, unhealthy coastal swamp and needed to get a breath of fresh mountain air. Paul's letter to the Galatians referring to his arrival in Galatia (4:13), could imply this. But, for whatever reason, here in Perga Mark turned back to Jerusalem, and Barnabas and Paul went on, up to Antioch in Pisidia.

THE WAY NORTH

From Perga, there were three possible routes, approximately following three roads still in use today, towards Yalvac.

1   The west route via Attalia and Isparta, east of Lake Egridir – which we shall take, on the main road – then a Roman road.
2   A route from Perga due north, up the Kestros, to the town of Egridir then round the east side of the lake – probably Paul's route on this occasion.
3   A Roman road east to Side, linking with a second Roman road up to Lake Beysehir, round the east side of that lake. Not the most direct route, but Roman roads all the way.

By *any* route, through the Taurus Mountains to the Inner Plateau, 3,000 feet high, a journey of at least 150 miles, could have taken six days' travelling!

Scripture References:
Acts 13:13 and 14
      14:24–26

13

ANTIOCH IN PISIDIA

It was probably in the high summer of the year 46 that Paul,
Barnabas and John Mark, Barnabas' nephew, landed at
Perga after their exhausting tour of Cyprus. In a dispassion-
ate twenty words, Luke, in Acts 13:13 and 14, records
briefly their arrival on the mainland, the mysterious withdrawal of John Mark and the departure of the two older
men for the inland Roman colony of Pisidian Antioch.

HIGH AND HEALTHY

The garrison town was high up on a plateau, 3,280 feet
above the Mediterranean, and 150 miles and six days' travel
from the coastal plain. Just why Paul and Barnabas undertook this perilous journey, rather than visit the many
townships along the coastline, is not clear. If their journey
marked a change of plan, then that could have been a
reason for Mark's sudden return to Jerusalem. Perhaps he
had anticipated working along the chain of Greek ports,
rather than a trek up the Taurus range to a Roman colonial
city.

William Ramsey was the first to suggest an explanation,
rooted in the climate of the Pamphylian plain in mid-
summer and linking Paul's reference in Galatians 4:12–14.
Here, Paul commented on the friendliness of the Galatians,
'from the very beginning when illness gave me the opportunity to preach the good news to you'. And again, 'you

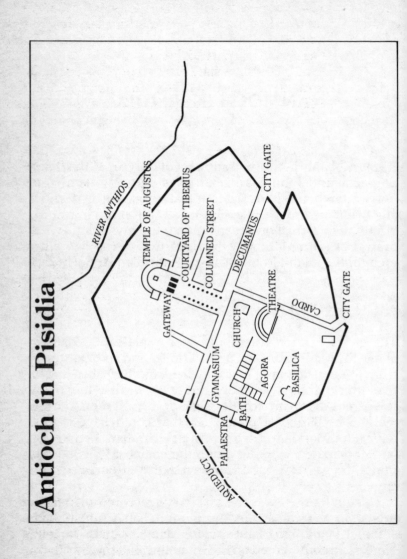

Antioch in Pisidia

RIVER ANTHIOS

TEMPLE OF AUGUSTUS

COURTYARD OF TIBERIUS

COLUMNED STREET

CITY GATE

DECUMANUS

GATEWAY

THEATRE

CARDO

CITY GATE

CHURCH

GYMNASIUM

BATH

AGORA

BASILICA

PALAESTRA

AQUEDUCT

never showed the least sign of being revolted or disgusted by my disease, that was such a trial for you'. Whether dysentery or malaria, both so common in the steaming heat of the coastal plain, Paul might well have needed a convalescence in the healthier highlands.

The Romans had established the province of Galatia in 25 B.C. Antioch, at the junction of the three regions, Pisidia to the west, Phrygia to the north and Lycaonia to the south, was an ideal base from which to subdue the mountain tribes.

Paul and Barnabas must have reached Antioch some time in August. There was a synagogue of Hellenistic Jews with a composite audience, as was obvious from Paul's opening address: 'Men of Israel *and* you that fear God, hearken.' Beyond the prayer hall, through the Gentiles' Courtyard, there was a strong non-Jewish congregation. It was this section that was so impressed by Paul's address that they petitioned for a special address on the next Sabbath to the Gentiles. Literally 'almost the whole city' gathered to hear it. But inevitably Jewish liberalism had its limitations and the Jewish congregation felt jealous and argumentative.

FAMILIAR PATTERNS

At this point Paul and Barnabas spoke out boldly: 'It was necessary that the word should first be spoken to you. Seeing ye thrust it from you and judge yourselves unworthy of eternal life, lo, we turn to the Gentiles.' A number of Gentiles believed, but the more nationalist Jews 'stirred up persecution against Paul and Barnabas, and cast them out of their borders'.

Codex Bezae adds that they 'stirred up great affliction and persecution'. Paul's enumeration of his sufferings in 2 Corinthians 11, includes being beaten three times with the rods of Roman lictors – a magistrate's punishment. On the whole it is therefore probable that both at Antioch, and later at Lystra, the 'persecution' included a lictor's beating.

Certainly, the third beating was at Philippi about the year
50, and 2 Corinthians was written only four years later.

Antioch showed Paul's world on one small stage and set
a familiar pattern for the rest of his ministry. Jews were
usually divided between those with ecumenical or Hellenistic leanings and those of more rigid views, who resisted
any modification of doctrine, like the Pharisees; and those
who saw advantage in collaborating with the Roman
authorities, like the Sadducees. It was so easy to charge
such popular newcomers with disturbing the harmony and
security of the state, an issue on which Romans were
naturally sensitive.

Nevertheless, in the course of perhaps several months'
stay 'many heard the word and believed', before Paul and
Barnabas moved on, to Iconium – leaving this staggering
challenge still ringing in their ears: 'My brothers, I want you
to realise that it is through Jesus that forgiveness of your
sins is proclaimed. Through him, justification from all sins
which the Law of Moses was unable to justify is offered to
every believer. So be careful – or what the prophets say will
happen to you:

> "Cast your eyes around you, mockers;
> be amazed and perish!
> For I am doing something in your own days
> that you would not believe if you were to be told of it."'

(Habakkuk 1:5)

Of Antioch in St Paul's day, little remains but a vast
many-arched Roman aqueduct.

Scripture References:
Acts 13:14–52

14

ICONIUM, SCRIPTURAL AND APOCRYPHAL

The manuscripts of Acts 14:1–6 vary and the narrative is obscure. Paul and Barnabas address crowds of both Jews and Greeks, of whom many believe – as at Antioch. Disaffected Jews, however, stir up bitter opposition to the apostles. Then, an early gloss adds that the apostles remained a long time preaching boldly with marked success. Finally, the result is that the populace is divided – part with the Jews, part with the apostles. Threatened with persecution and stoning, the apostles flee into Lycaonia. No assessment of success is added, as in Antioch.

Perhaps the difference of response is natural. Antioch was the governing centre of a wide area. Iconium was only an insignificant town in the same district. When they left Iconium, however, they crossed the frontier to a new region and a new sphere of work.

When they set out from Antioch, they travelled on the Roman road linking the two garrison towns of Antioch and Lystra. About halfway down the Roman road at Misthia, they turned off due east to Iconium, then called Claudiconium, an honour bestowed by the Emperor Claudius during an administrative reorganisation of the province. The city, however, remained Greek and was not Romanised.

In a late second-century apocryphal 'Acts of Paul and Thekla' – which may yet contain some genuine tradition – Paul reflects on the persecution and afflictions he endured at Antioch, Iconium and Lystra. This was in contrast to his acknowledgment in his letter to the Galatians of many acts of kindness. One such was performed (*sic* the Acts of Paul and Thekla) on this very road, by a citizen of Iconium, called Onesiphorus. This man went to meet Paul on his way from Antioch, at the crossroads at Misthia. Like any host meeting a notable guest, Onesiphorus had a description of Paul – whom of course he had never met before. He was looking for: 'a man small in size with meeting eyebrows, with a rather large nose, bald, bow-legged, strongly built, full of grace who at times seemed to have the face of an angel'!

Onesiphorus met Paul, who accepted his hospitality and taught sitting in the courtyard of his house, overlooked from a rather larger house next door. So it was that Thekla, the daughter of Onesiphorus' neighbour, from her window heard and was fascinated by Paul's message and became his devoted follower. The apocryphal tale of her sufferings and miraculous deliverances followed.

If verse four of Acts 14 is accepted, Paul may have stayed at Iconium through the winter, longer than in either Antioch or Lystra. For Luke, Iconium seems to have been a minor link in a larger chain. Antioch had been the scene of a major doctrinal statement and review of Hebrew scriptures, resulting in a historic 'turn to the Gentiles'. Lystra was to hear the first address to a specifically Gentile audience, completely outside the Jewish tradition.

The pattern of events in Iconium was necessarily rather different, for it was a Greek town with no Roman ruling power to which the Jews could protest (as at Antioch). In this situation, the Jews stirred up the Gentiles and the city was divided in its response to Paul's message. Riot resulted and no doubt a hint to Paul to move on, before any court proceedings. Consequently he was able to stage a quiet return to the city on his way back from Lystra and Derbe, when the matter was forgotten.

Any remains of Greek Iconium were buried beneath the medieval buildings, mosques, palaces and mansions of a sultan's city of the eleventh to fourteenth century. From here, the Turks harassed the tottering eastern empire at Constantinople and boasted of Konya's beauty: 'See all the world, but see Konya!'

Two early myths seek to explain the name Iconium: one recounts a story of the flood, whose waters receded at the command of Zeus, after which Prometheus and Athena made images (*eikones* in Greek) of mud into which the winds breathed life. And so the world was repopulated. The second legend told how Perseus came and conquered the countryside by displaying the Gorgon's head, which turned all who looked to stone. (This is recorded on Iconian coins.) A certain village presented Perseus with an image, or *eikon*, of the Gorgon's head. On the site of the village, he founded the city of Iconium.

Today Konya is a religious centre, famous for its Tekke, or monastery of Whirling Dervishes, the tomb of whose founder – Mevlana – is the most striking monument in the city. Mevlana was a thirteenth-century Sufi poet and philosopher, who induced an ecstatic state of universal love by the practice of whirling round and round. For six centuries, the Tekke was a centre of mystic Sufi culture until banned and dissolved by Ataturk in 1925.

Ala-et-Tin (the original Alladin?) Park and Mosque are on the site of the Greek acropolis and later Seljuk citadel.

Scripture References:
Acts 14:1–7

15

LYSTRA AND DERBE

Twenty-three miles south of Iconium is a sizeable hill and obvious military vantage-point. Not surprisingly it became a Roman garrison town and colony from which to control the southern highlands of Lycaonia – though not so distinguished as its sister colony of Antioch in Pisidia.

This was a different administrative district from Iconium, and not likely to have been on Paul's planned itinerary, but rather an escape route from Iconium. Roman rule and civic pride were strong in Lystra, as witness the amount of Latin in surviving inscriptions. But, in other respects, both Lystra and Derbe were more primitive than most places visited by Paul, in that they were oriental towns rather than Greek cities. They were local market towns, whose peasants spoke an ancient dialect, the native language of Lycaonia. Among the residents were also the Latin-speaking Italian colonists, and the Greek-speaking and Hebrew-speaking trades folk.

Perhaps, among these last was the family of Lois, mother of Eunice and grandmother of Timothy, all of whom were converted by Paul on his first visit in the year 46. Timothy certainly knew of Paul's subsequent stoning (2 Tim. 3:11). When Paul passed through Lystra, on his second journey, four years later, he collected Timothy from his home and family to be his lieutenant in evangelism among the Jews. Paul took Timothy – whose father was a Greek and whose mother was a Jewess – and circumcised him to convince the Jews of his adherence to the Jewish Law. Writing in 2

Timothy 1:5, Paul says: 'I am reminded of your sincere faith, a faith that dwelt first in your grandmother Lois, then your mother Eunice, and now I am sure dwells in you.' And in 2 Timothy 3:14, he urges them to 'Continue in what you have learned and have firmly believed . . .' Timothy was to become the first Bishop of Ephesus.

Paul and Barnabas must have reached the market town of Lystra that same night, when the chatter in the local Lycao-nian dialect, the bargaining in stumbling Greek and all the hubbub of the market had ceased for the night. There is no trace of a synagogue in Lystra, which has never been properly excavated, but the apostles probably found hos-pitality in the Jewish community. Judging by Timothy's mixed parentage, the Jewish community may have been fairly liberal and it was not the Jews who put an end to the apostles' visit but the 'locals'.

It began with Paul preaching, probably in the town forum, the story of Christ crucified and risen. A cripple, lame from birth, caught Paul's eye as he listened. Paul perceived his faith and called on him to 'stand up' on his feet. The man jumped up and began to walk – to the amazement of the crowd, who proclaimed Barnabas and Paul to be Zeus, the father of all the gods, and Hermes (or Mercury) his messenger. Luke's report is confirmed by archaeological evidence that these were the patron deities of the Lycaonian countryside. Third-century inscriptions, one recording the dedication to Zeus of a statue to Hermes, the other mentioning 'priests of Zeus', and a stone altar to 'The Hearer of Prayer and Hermes' have been found. The last is to be seen in the Konya Museum.

It was the priests of Zeus 'outside the gate' of Lystra who proposed that the people should offer the apostles sacrifice, so presumably the Temple of Zeus was out of town.

The extraordinary, emotional response to the healing and preaching power of the apostles is explained by a legend preserved by the Roman poet Ovid, fifty years before Paul and Barnabas arrived. Ovid had put into verse all the stories he could find about transformation or metamorphosis. His collection became famous and in his eighth book, he told the story of Philemon and Baucis, who 'entertained angels unawares'.

In the Phrygian hill-country [writes Ovid], an oak and a linden tree stand side by side. Not far away is a marsh, once habitable land, but now the watery haunt of divers and coots. To this place came Zeus in the guise of a mortal, and along with him came Atlas' grandson. To a thousand homes they came seeking a resting-place; a thousand homes were thatched with straw and reeds from the marsh. There, a poor old married couple, Philemon and Baucis, married in that same cottage in their youth, had grown old together, bearing all their poverty in a spirit of contentment.

The heavenly visitors stooped low under the cottage doorway. Baucis threw a coverlet over the rough wooden bench and stirred the dying ashes of the fire and threw on it some of their precious fuel. Philemon cut a cabbage from the garden and boiled it with a lump of bacon, from under the rafters. The table was laid with cream cheese, eggs, nuts, apples and dried dates to make a little feast with humble fare. The wine bowl, as it is emptied, refills of its own accord and the couple suddenly recognise their guests and beg forgiveness for their poor hospitality. They try to catch their favourite goose to do greater honour to their guests, but it eludes their shaky chase and seeks refuge with Zeus and Hermes.

This is the omen. The gods rise and proclaim vengeance on the wicked, uncaring district. They lead the old couple up a nearby hill and, before their horrified eyes, the land is flooded and their little cottage alone remains. Then, the cottage itself was transformed into a temple with marble columns. Its thatch became the golden roof. As for the old pair, all they asked was 'Let us be your priests, to guard your temple. And since we have spent our lives together let the same hour take us, that I may never see my wife's grave, nor be buried by her.'

And so it was. One day as they talked of old times, Philemon became an oak and Baucis, his wife, a linden tree. A reading of Ovid's text could fix the site near Lystra, but geography is irrelevant in such folklore and legend. The 'Phrygian hill-country' is near enough. As Abraham entertained angels unawares at Mamre, so once more the gods had come down 'in the likeness of men' with healing in their hands. At this second advent, the opportunity was not to be missed. Imagination soon became ecstasy.

Of course Barnabas, Uncle Barnabas with a spade beard, was the very figure of Zeus and his mercurial little messenger Paul was a natural Hermes. It would have been funny, if it had not nearly proved fatal! The apostles' inhibition of worship broke the spell. 'Hosanna' turned to 'Crucify' and roses into stones. Under their passionate pelting, Paul nearly perished. Derbe, down the road, was the only escape route, but of that town nothing but the site can even be guessed, except for a circular inscription to an early Bishop Michael of Derbe, now in the Karaman Museum.

NB Routes to a) Lystra from Konya: Seydisehir road to Hatip. Road to Akoren 23 miles.

  b) Derbe from Karaman: Aranci road 14 miles. Turn left to Akcasehir, at Ekinozu village enquire track to Derbe, 3 miles through fields to mound.

Scripture References:
Acts 14:6–23
    16:1–3

Part Four:

SECOND MISSIONARY
JOURNEY

Pergamum

1. Sacred Way
2. Propylaeum
3. Library
4. Porticos
5. Theatre
6. Springs
7. Latrines
8. Subvault of portico
9. Cryptoporticus
10. Pump Room
11. Temple of Zeus-Asklepeios

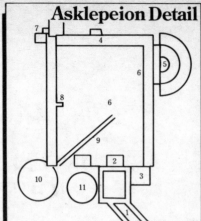

Asklepeion Detail

7
4
5
6
6
8
9
2
3
10
11
1

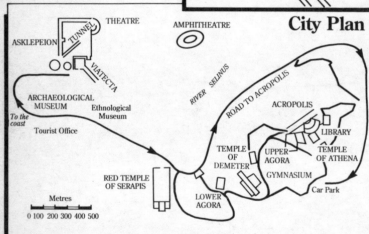

City Plan

THEATRE
AMPHITHEATRE
TUNNEL
ASKLEPEION
VIATECTA
RIVER SELINUS
ROAD TO ACROPOLIS
ARCHAEOLOGICAL MUSEUM
Ethnological Museum
ACROPOLIS
To the coast
Tourist Office
LIBRARY
TEMPLE OF DEMETER
UPPER AGORA
TEMPLE OF ATHENA
GYMNASIUM
RED TEMPLE OF SERAPIS
LOWER AGORA
Car Park

Metres
0 100 200 300 400 500

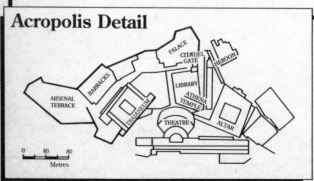

Acropolis Detail

PALACE
CITADEL GATE
HEROON
BARRACKS
ARSENAL TERRACE
LIBRARY
TRAIANEUM
ATHENA TEMPLE
THEATRE
ALTAR

0   40   80
Metres

16

PERGAMUM

'Easily the most spectacular city in Asia Minor,' said Professor Ramsey. 'The one city in the land which forced the exclamation "a royal city"!'

The acropolis stands on a hill 900 feet above the surrounding plain, fifteen miles inland and two miles north of the Caicus River in southern Mysia.

On the upper acropolis are the palace, the library, the Athena Temple, the Trajaneum, the barracks and the arsenal terrace. On a second level, eighty feet lower, is the site of the great Altar of Zeus. The theatre is on the steep southern slope with a marvellous view over the plain.

Along the north-east slopes were the three major gymnasia. The healing shrine, the Asklepeion, was on the plain.

NEW TESTAMENT REFERENCES

What was the 'throne of Satan', Revelation 2:13, mentioned after the introduction of the seven letters to the Churches of Asia, Revelation 1:11?

Was it the great Altar of Zeus, or the general appearance of the hilltop acropolis, or the cult of Asklepeios?

HISTORICAL BACKGROUND

On the death of Alexander, Lysimachus controlled the region around Pergamum. His rebellious treasurer

Philetaerus established the Pergamum dynasty of the Attalids in 283 B.C. He dedicated the sanctuary to Athena and hoped to make Pergamum the Athens of Asia Minor, as did his successors Eumenes and Attalus I.

These first three kings, 283–197 B.C., had to repel the marauding Galatians. Attalus set up statues of defeated Galatian warriors killing themselves. His successor Eumenes II commemorated his victories by erecting the Altar of Zeus. He also built the library. His successor Attalus II presented the magnificent stoa (380 feet long) in the agora at Athens – now rebuilt and serving as a museum. He also built, outside the citadel gate at Pergamum, a sanctuary, a shrine in honour of his royal predecessors or heroes.

EXCAVATIONS

In 1878, eight years after Schlieman's excavations at Troy, German archaeologists began to reveal the upper city of Pergamum and the middle and lower terraces from 1900. From 1927 to 1935, the arsenals, the Red Basilica and Asklepeion were disclosed. It was now possible to trace the development of a third-century B.C. fortress into a royal city, on a succession of terraces grouped around a steeply raked theatre.

Along the main street curving up the acropolis, the excavations have found that many new buildings had replaced earlier Hellenistic structures during the first century, possibly after an earthquake. At this time, the sewers and drains were cleaned out. The water supply and drainage systems were impressively engineered. The supply was forced up the hill for two miles through metal pipes. In the reign of Claudius a new drinking-water pipe was installed near the baths. Some of us may know the impressive water tower and aqueduct at Laodicea.

A well-preserved odeion has been uncovered and restored. Also restored and next to the odeion is the 'Marble

Hall', a shrine to a departed hero. Nearby was a food shop, with the remains of meals found in a pit.

THE ALTAR OF ZEUS

The word altar is misleading. It is a monumental colonnaded court in the form of a horseshoe 120 feet by 112 feet. The podium, or platform, of the altar was eighteen feet high. The great frieze, which ran at the base of the structure for 446 feet, depicted a battle of the gods and giants. It must have been one of the greatest works of Hellenistic art. This, reconstructed, is the centre-piece of the Pergamum Museum in East Berlin. Third only to the British Museum and the Louvre, the East Berlin Museum houses, among other reconstructions, the Ishtar Gate of Nebuchadnezzar's Babylon. At Pergamum itself remains only the base of the Altar of Zeus, while the top (like a mini Victor Emmanuel wedding cake monument) is in Berlin.

THE LIBRARY

On the top of the acropolis, the library was second only to that in Alexandria. When Ptolemy V refused to sell papyrus (from Egypt) to Eumenes II, the Pergamenes used sheep- and goatskins to produce parchment – for which the Latin word became *pergamentium*. When Mark Antony offered the library to Cleopatra, it held 200,000 volumes. The reading-room measured fifty by forty feet. Holes in the wall indicate the system of bookshelves. The main room could have stored only 12,500 rolls. The rest must have been held elsewhere.

THE THEATRE

South of the library and Temple of Athena is the steeply slanted theatre, accommodating 10,000 spectators. The

scene building is 122 feet below the top seats. The portico/
promenade below the theatre was 245 feet long and the
panorama from the theatre is breathtaking.

THE GYMNASIA

The word gymnasium comes from the Greek word for the
place where athletic exercises were practised 'in the nude'
(*gymnos* = naked). The gymnasium was also a lecture-
room. Socrates, Plato and Aristotle all taught in gymnasia.
In the Roman period, the gymnasium served as a centre of
educational and social life. Within the community at Pergamum there were at least seven with the multiple functions
of civic centre, club house, leisure centre, school, place of
worship. Wealthier citizens were expected to share their
wealth for civic purposes – and were rewarded with the
honour of statues and inscriptions (Erastus at Corinth). At
Pergamum, the three major gymnasia were on adjoining
terraces: the upper for men over twenty, the middle for
teenagers and the lower for little boys. A list of promotions
from the second century would suggest a total population
of 12,000!

THE IMPERIAL CULT

Pergamum was one of the first Asian cities to welcome
Rome as an ally. In 133 B.C. Attalus II bequeathed his
kingdom to the Romans. Julius Caesar was honoured here
with a statue as early as 63 B.C. Even when Pergamum was
replaced by Ephesus as 'capital of the Roman province',
Pergamum remained the focal point of the worship of the
Roman emperors. Here the first Asian Temple of Augustus
was the one centre of the imperial religion for the whole
province. A second was later built at Smyrna and a third
at Ephesus, but they were secondary to the original at
Pergamum.

The outstanding imperial sanctuary was the Trajaneum, built by Hadrian in honour of his adoptive father, on the top of the acropolis – the most splendid monument erected to Trajan anywhere. Recent excavations have revealed a left hand and foot, probably part of a colossal statue of Trajan or Hadrian. Pergamum, like Ephesus and Artemis, received the title of 'Neokoros' or 'temple-keeper'.

When John, Seer of Patmos, wrote the Revelation at the time of the first temple, whose presence and ritual was enough to make Rome's authority oppressively apparent in the city, the imperial power of the 'one who holds a two-edged sword' challenged Christian faith in this cathedral centre of the state religion. Paul may have hoped that the empire would receive Christ, but Christians at Pergamum lived in the presence of a dire alternative, 'where Satan's seat was'.

Paganism at Pergamum lay in three strata:

1 The ancient *Anatolian* worship of Dionysus, god of wine, and of Demeter, goddess of grain and growth (whose mystery rites must have resembled those of Eleusis) and also Asklepeios, god of healing.

    Snakes and the handling of reptiles were associated with the cult of Dionysus and particularly of Asklepeios.

The drawing on the previous page shows a column at the Entrance to the Asklepeion, of snakes drinking milk, which when drunk helped to heal human patients. A Pergamene coin shows the Emperor Caracalla, spear in hand, before a great serpent twined around a tree. He is giving a salute to the serpent. Christians associated the serpent with Satan and found the serpent-infested Asklepeion diabolical.

2   The snake symbol is also present in the second stratum. Zeus and Athena represent the coming of the *Greeks* to Asia. The Greek traveller Pausanius (whom some of us have met on Mars Hill) described the huge altar to Zeus, built to commemorate the defeat of a Gallic invasion centuries before. The wandering Celts gave their name to Galatia. Pergamum was strong enough to drive them away and celebrated the deliverance with the altar to Zeus. The main frieze around the altar depicted a battle between the gods of Olympus and serpent-tailed giants.

3   The topmost strata represented the Roman period of the imperial cult. Perhaps Antipas, the faithful martyr of Revelation 2:13, was the first to suffer, dying by burning in a brazen bull in the time of Domitian. Christ and Caesar were in a head-on collision, which could be disregarded perhaps, but the Roman demands were unavoidable. It was literally 'sacrifice or die'. The Nicolaitans in Pergamum were the compromisers, the 'thin-end-of-the-wedgers'. The apostles saw with devastating clarity how *any* compromise was bound to lead to a landslide of faith and morals, but they remained firm, faithful, lonely and execrated within this threatening community.

Scripture References:
Revelation 1:11
          2:12–17

17

TROAS AND ASSOS

LOCATION

Strabo describes Assos as 'strong and well-fortified, with a harbour formed by a great mole – a notable city'. Assos stood on a scenic site on the Adramyttium Gulf, north of the island of Lesbos and on the south coast of the Troad, forty-five miles south of Troy.

On his second missionary journey, Paul was forbidden by the Holy Spirit to preach the word in Asia. 'When they reached the frontier of Mysia, they thought to cross it into Bithynia, but as the Spirit of Jesus would not allow them, they went through Mysia and came down to Troas' (*sic* Jerusalem Bible, Acts 16:6, 7).

The routes available and his choice of Troas suggest he already knew where he was going and that Troas was the first stage of a journey to Macedonia and beyond. This would make the vision of the Macedonian Stranger a confirmation of Paul's existing resolve. Perhaps Luke, who had travelled from Macedonia and met Paul in Troas, was himself the Macedonian Stranger. (Jerome says he was from Antioch; Antioch and Philippi were neighbouring Roman colonies.)

The Greco-Roman port of Alexandria Troas, a key port in New Testament times, was ten miles south of Homer's Ancient Troy. Alexandria Troas is mentioned in Acts 16:8–11 and 20:5–6, 2 Corinthians 2:12 and 2 Timothy 4:13. Until

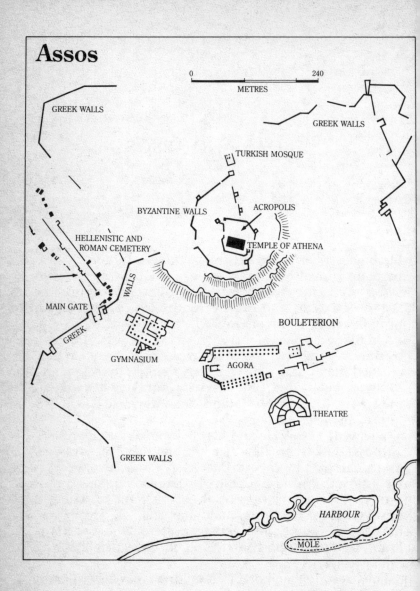

Assos

0 _____ 240
METRES

GREEK WALLS

GREEK WALLS

TURKISH MOSQUE

BYZANTINE WALLS

ACROPOLIS

TEMPLE OF ATHENA

HELLENISTIC AND
ROMAN CEMETERY

WALLS

MAIN GATE

GREEK

BOULETERION

GYMNASIUM

AGORA

THEATRE

GREEK WALLS

HARBOUR

MOLE

1870, Ancient Troy was mistakenly sited at Alexandria Troas.

In the middle of his third missionary journey, some ten years later, Paul stayed some time at Troas, impatiently awaiting Titus' return from his 'corrective' visit to Corinth. In contrast to Corinth, Paul found Troas 'wide open for my work there in the Lord', but soon left for Macedonia to intercept Titus (2 Cor. 2:12, 13).

Luke (20:3–5) describes how Paul spent three months in Greece before returning via Macedonia to Troas, and spent a week there before sailing home. On the Sunday night, Paul preached at the Eucharist long into the night. 'A number of lights were lit in the upstairs room where we were assembled, and as Paul went on and on, a young man called Eutychus who was sitting on the window-sill grew drowsy and was overcome by sleep and fell to the ground three floors below, where he was picked up dead.' Luke goes on to describe his resuscitation by Paul, who returned upstairs to preach until day-break. Luke's fascination with the medical miracle allocated it eight verses, compared with three verses for Paul's three months in Greece!

Wanting to bid his friends at Troas a final farewell, Paul sent Luke and the others on ahead by sea, and walked or rode on his own to meet them at the harbour of Assos. (Little remains of Troas today and its harbour is a lagoon, but the road is still there and visible near Assos.)

Some six or seven years later, after his release from imprisonment in Rome, Paul was again in Troas. Here he was, perhaps in the year 64, finally re-arrested and sent back to Rome – in such a hurry that he left his cloak with Carpus together with all his precious note-books (2 Tim. 4:13 – probably the last chapter he wrote!).

The city of Assos was founded by immigrants from northern Greece about 1000 B.C. By 600 B.C., it had become the most important city in the Troad, with a population of about 12,000.

HISTORY

It fell to the Persians, with Sardis, in 546 B.C. – but regained its freedom on the Greek victory, at Mycale, in 479, when its population had been reduced to 4,000.

In the fourth century B.C., Hermeias, a former eunuch and slave, who had been a pupil of Plato, became the ruler of Assos. On the death of Plato, Aristotle had hoped to succeed him as head of the Academy, but was disappointed and accepted the invitation of Hermeias to join his court at Assos. Aristotle married the ruler's niece, Pythias, and continued his studies in zoology, botany and biology under the patronage of Hermeias.

In 342 B.C., a Greek general serving the Persian king, Artaxerxes III, seized Hermeias, because he was an ally of Philip of Macedon. Hermeias was crucified by the Persian king and Aristotle composed a poem in his honour, setting up a statue to him at Delphi.

Cleanthes, successor to Zeno as leader of the Stoics in Athens, was born in Assos in about 330 B.C. When St Paul, on Mars Hill, quoted 'for we are all his offspring', he was quoting from the 'Hymn to Zeus', written by Cleanthes of Assos (Acts 17:28).

ARCHAEOLOGY

Despite the pillaging of the city's cut stones by the Turks in 1864 for the construction of new docks at Istanbul, the fourth-century city walls are still in a marvellous state of preservation. Perhaps the most complete fortification in the Greek world, the north tower of the main gateway still stands fifty feet high. The firing slits in the tower were used for bolt-projecting catapults.

On top of the 700-feet high acropolis was the impressive Temple of Athena. Bits of its frieze can be seen in museums at Istanbul, Boston and in the Louvre.

The agora was flanked by the north stoa, on the acropolis

side, 380 feet long and on the south or sea-side by a
somewhat shorter stoa, which was built in three storeys –
with shops on the middle floor and bathrooms below. East
of the north stoa was the bema or rostrum and, a little
further on, the bouleterion or council chamber. Both these
buildings are a mixture of Doric and Ionic styles. The south
stoa overlooked the theatre, which in turn looked out over
the harbour. In 1826, there were forty rows of seats visible.

On the death of the last King of Pergamum, in 133 B.C.,
Assos, with the rest of western Asia Minor, passed to the
Romans. Many Romans lived in Assos and left their inscrip-
tions. The imperial cult prevailed. On a stoa near the
gymnasium, an inscription read: 'The priest of the god
Caesar Augustus, himself likewise hereditary king, priest
of Zeus Homonoos, and gymnasiarch, Quintus Lollius
Philetairos, have dedicated the stoa to the god Caesar
Augustus and the people.'

Similarly, the donor's wife also dedicated a bath to Julia
Aphrodite in honour of the Empress Livia: 'Lollia Anti-
ochis, wife of Quintus Lollius Philetairos, first of women,
who was queen in accordance with ancestral customs,
dedicated this bath and its belongings to Julia Aphrodite
and the people [of Rome].'

Augustus had hoped to be succeeded by his grandsons,
Gaius and Lucius, but Lucius died in A.D. 2 and Gaius was
killed in A.D. 4. Numerous statues of the two grandsons
have been found in Asia Minor, including one of Gaius in
Assos.

When Caligula became emperor in A.D. 37, five citizens
from Assos went to Rome to represent their city and
sacrifice there to the Capitoline Jupiter.

Scripture References:
Acts 16:7–11
        20:4–14
2 Corinthians 2:12 and 13
2 Timothy 4:13

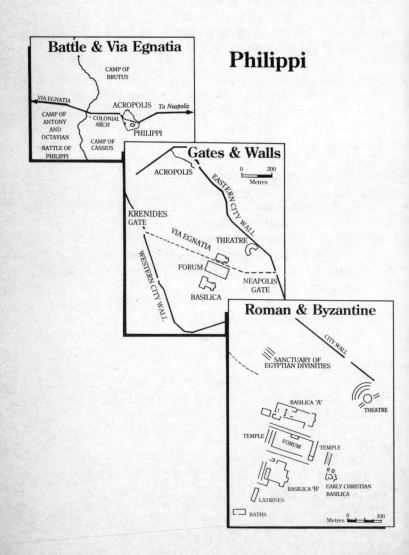

Philippi

Battle & Via Egnatia

CAMP OF BRUTUS

VIA EGNATIA

ACROPOLIS   *To Neapolis*

CAMP OF ANTONY AND OCTAVIAN

· COLONIAL ARCH

PHILIPPI

BATTLE OF PHILIPPI

CAMP OF CASSIUS

Gates & Walls

0   200
Metres

ACROPOLIS

EASTERN CITY WALL

KRENIDES GATE

VIA EGNATIA

THEATRE

WESTERN CITY WALL

FORUM

BASILICA

NEAPOLIS GATE

Roman & Byzantine

CITY WALL

SANCTUARY OF EGYPTIAN DIVINITIES

THEATRE

BASILICA 'A'

TEMPLE   FORUM   TEMPLE

BASILICA 'B'   EARLY CHRISTIAN BASILICA

LATRINES

☐ BATHS

0   100
Metres

18

PHILIPPI

As if in confirmation of Paul's good intention to take the gospel to Europe, favourable winds enabled his ship to cross from Troas to Neapolis – a distance of 120 miles – in forty-eight hours. It took him five days on the return journey.

A stone in the churchyard of St Nicholas marks the traditional place of his landing, not so impossible when we remember how the shoreline receded. Originally a church dedicated to St Paul, converted during the Turkish occupation into a mosque, it was restored and dedicated by the fishermen of Kavalla to their patron saint Nicholas of Myra.

In the time of Paul, the town was called Neapolis (New City), and in the Christian period Christoupolis (City of Christ). One of the Greek bishops in the UK has the title of 'Bishop of Christoupolis'. In the Turkish occupation, in recognition of it being in both Roman and Ottoman times the terminus of a 'pony express' postal service, the town was called Kavalla – Vulgar Latin for 'horse'.

If he stayed the night, Paul would have climbed to the old town on the rocky promontory to the north, where the shell of the citadel stands today. Maybe he would have seen the Roman predecessor of the three-tier aqueduct that stands today, built in the design of its predecessor but by the initiative of Suleiman the Magnificent in the sixteenth century.

The modern visitor to the old town must not miss two places of interest. One is the 'Imaret', a neglected old almshouse with a colonnade under eight domes, which sheltered no less than 300 divans behind lattice screens. No wonder the Turks called it 'The Home of the Lazy Ones'! The other is the birthplace of Mehmet Ali, an Albanian farmer born in 1769, who became Pasha of Egypt at the age of thirty and founded a dynasty that only died with Farouk. The statue and rambling town house, cared for by the Egyptian government, conjure up visions of eunuchs and harems, stallions and scimitars.

No doubt Paul followed the Via Egnatia over the skyline, all the nine miles to Philippi. As he topped the ridge overlooking the harbour, he would have seen a conical hill rising from a fertile plain. This constituted an obvious vantage-point occupied by a town called Krenides, until fortified and renamed Philippi by Philip of Macedon in the middle of the fourth century B.C. Philip needed an observation point from which to protect the goldfields of Mount Pangaeon.

In the year 42 B.C., following the murder of Julius Caesar, this marshy plain was the scene of a clash between the army of the young Octavian – destined to become the Emperor Augustus – with Mark Antony, and the opposing forces of Brutus and Cassius. Shakespeare well depicts the gloomy portents and omens behind a military defeat which led to the suicides first of Cassius and then of Brutus, whose head Octavian sent to Rome to adorn the statue of Caesar. When the victorious allies met at Actium, Octavian defeated Antony and transformed Philippi into a Roman colony of veterans. This bustling barracks of legionaries, this Latin-speaking 'Little Rome', soon achieved self-government. Even Luke's account reflects a touch of civic pride, as he calls it 'the Leading City of Macedonia'. It was this community which Paul was to visit and which was to occupy such a place in both the sufferings and affections of the apostle.

I thank my God whenever I think of you – every time I pray for all of you. I pray with joy. It is only natural that I should feel like this towards you all, since you have shared the privileges which have been mine, both my chains and my work establishing the gospel. You have a permanent place in my heart. God knows how much I miss you all, loving you as Christ Jesus loves you. [The opening of Paul's letter to Philippi.]

What letter could begin with more love and affectionate remembrance? But what a story lies behind that letter – and it all began with a dream!

When at Troas – near ancient Troy on the Turkish mainland – Paul had in that night a vision of a 'Man of Macedonia' from over the Aegean in northern Greece. The man just stood there in the doorway and begged Paul: 'Come to Macedonia and help us!'

The story is told by Luke in Acts 16, for Luke had just met Paul for the first time and been recruited to the team of Paul, Silas and Timothy. The Acts narrative changes at that point for the first time from 'they' to 'we' and continues all the way back to Jerusalem and even on to Rome some years later: 'That same night' – Luke writes – 'Paul was utterly convinced that God was calling us to proclaim the good news to Macedonia.'

They searched for a ship and sailed, probably at the end of July in the year 50. Even the winds were in their favour and within two days' sailing they were off the island of Samothrace. That was where ninety years earlier Brutus buried Cassius after their defeat at Philippi by Mark Antony and Augustus, who thus revenged the murder of Caesar. The second night out they landed at the port of Neapolis, the little harbour tucked under the mountain range below Philippi. Next day they climbed the nine miles over the hills on the great Via Egnatia, the Roman highway that linked the Aegean to the Adriatic.

Paul and his friends found lodgings, but few Jews and no synagogue, so his first port of call in Europe lacked the usual launching-pad for preaching. There was, however, a devout woman called Lydia from Asia Minor, in the purple dye trade. When Paul and his companions went to pray and preach outside the gate by the riverside, Lydia accepted Paul's message and was converted. She and her household were baptised in the River Gangites and insisted on the visitors coming to stay at her house. It was to this little Christian community, which by then had its own elders and deacons, that Paul was to write some years later with such affection.

Just when Paul thought he had established a bridgehead – daily going down to the river to the place of prayer to preach the good news of Jesus – an unexpected incident put an end to his stay in Philippi. A sooth-saying slave girl with an evil spirit began to follow Paul and Silas, continually calling out: 'These men are slaves of the Supreme God and are announcing to you the way of Salvation!' Luke discovered later that she had been a priestess (a 'pythoness') from the great shrine of Apollo at Delphi. She was now owned and exploited by a syndicate, who made considerable profit from her fortune-telling. Every day and all day she haunted them with her eerie proclamations, until Paul, as much for her sake as for his own relief, exorcised her in the name of Jesus Christ.

The girl was at once transformed and recovered her normality, but for her employers she was no longer of value as a medium and clairvoyant. She had been devalued into a common servant. Her owners had Paul and Silas arrested and hauled before the magistrates. Under pressure from the crowd, the magistrates had them stripped and flogged without trial. Now, the slave-owners' case was weak, but they wanted revenge. So, they charged: 'These men are causing a disturbance in our city.' The magistrates could indeed see the truth of this – but worse was to come: 'They are Jews too and teach customs which it is not lawful for us to practise *being Romans.*' And although Paul and Silas were themselves Romans, they never got the chance to be heard. Without formal sentence, but only 'on the nod', the lictors drew their rods, stripped the prisoners and lashed them up to the flogging posts. Any doubts about the guilt of the prisoners was soon dispersed by the sight of Paul's scarred and knotted back. As he put it: 'Whipped so many times almost to death. Five times I had the thirty-nine lashes from the Jews. Three times I have been beaten with rods, once stoned.' And now again the lictors worked with a will, the crowd roared and the blood spurted and their backs burnt like fire.

The magistrates stopped it before either collapsed, but the prisoners had to be half-carried up from the forum, across the road and into the prison built into the hillside under the acropolis. There, the gaoler – himself a Roman veteran – with instructions to guard them closely, assumed they were dangerous criminals, who would end up as galley slaves. Still naked, they were manhandled into one of the caves, stretched into the stocks and left for the night.

In a state of physical shock and acute discomfort – not to mention the pain and stiffening of their backs – they lay and shivered. As the shock and pain eased, the sense of outrage filled them, as Roman citizens in a Roman colony suffering Roman punishment and torture . . . then, gradually, they began to identify with the Roman sufferings of their Lord, and to pray and lift their praise to *Him*. Their voices rose in song: 'At the Name of Jesus, every knee should bow and every tongue acclaim Jesus Christ as Lord – to the glory of God the Father.'

Suddenly, the prison shook with an earthquake, dislodging their fetters, loosening the stocks and opening the doors of the gaol. The gaoler arrived with drawn sword to find the gates wide open and presumably his prisoners fled. He had no honourable choice but suicide, until a voice from inside called, 'Do yourself no harm. We are *all here*!' Calling for torches, the gaoler ran in to Paul and Silas, threw himself trembling at their feet and cried: 'What must I do to be saved?' 'Believe in the Lord Jesus, you and all your household too!' And so they preached and so he believed. Having washed their wounds, he and his family were all baptised.

At daylight the magistrates sent an order for their release, but Paul insisted that they came personally and escorted them openly from the prison. 'They flog Roman citizens in public and without trial. They throw us into prison and now they think they can push us out on the quiet! Do they? Oh no, let them come themselves!' The magistrates realised the enormity of their mistake. They understood the threat of complaint to Rome and the possibility of their own ruin. They led the apostles out of gaol with public honour and asked – as a favour – that Paul and his companions leave the colony, to avoid further breach of the peace.

The apostles called at Lydia's house to encourage the little Christian community and perhaps to introduce the gaoler and his family – then they set off across the plain to Thessalonica.

HOW TO SEE PHILIPPI TODAY

A visit to the site of Philippi today should include several distinct areas, though in what order will depend upon the size or energy of the group. A larger group will probably prefer to see the forum and later basilica ('B') south of the road, before crossing to the north to visit the prison, earlier basilica ('A'), acropolis and theatre. Here they are explained in chronological order.

From Kavalla both main road and ancient Via Egnatia, exactly parallel but separated by a few yards, enter the city walls at the Neapolis Gate from the east. They bisect the heart of the city across the north of the forum and out through the Krenides Gate, to the west.

Most of the sections of the city walls of Philip of Macedon (c. 350 B.C.) that survive are on the acropolis hill. The total city perimeter was nearly three miles. To that early period belong some 150 open-air shrines on the acropolis to a variety of deities including the Thracian equivalent of Artemis, Cybele the earth mother, Bacchus god of wine and the Egyptian gods. In the south-east slope is the Greek theatre, probably from the same times.

Descending the acropolis and crossing the roads, we

enter the Roman forum, whose main buildings are dated by inscriptions from the second century A.D., but which was certainly the site of the forum in St Paul's day. At the centre of the north side are four steps up to the bema, the tribunal or judgment seat, in front of which Paul and Silas appeared before the magistrates. The forum is a vast rectangle more than 100 yards long by 50 yards wide. In the corners nearest to the Via Egnatia were two Corinthian temples, on the west of the Emperor Antoninus Pius, on the east to his wife Faustina.

The Roman architect, Vitruvius, commented that prisons were sited beside or near the forum of a city. This would confirm the location of Paul's prison across the road from the north-west corner of the forum, not 100 yards from the bema, where they were flogged. There today, next to some steps up the acropolis, is a crypt or one-time cistern. In this cave, on its discovery in 1876, were murals of the imprisonment of Paul and Silas, of which only small fragments have survived exposure.

Four hundred years later, a great basilica stood on the terrace, cut between the road and the acropolis. It was orientated to enclose the prison within a colonnaded courtyard. This in turn led into an atrium and through a triple entrance into the narthex. The basilica, beyond, had a nave and two aisles leading up to a sanctuary with an apse flanked by truncated transepts. It must have looked magnificent in dazzling white marble. On the north side is a room with a beautiful mosaic floor and some murals, perhaps a baptistery or sacristy. The whole length of this huge complex was 130 yards by 50 yards wide, but within less than 100 years it was destroyed by earthquake.

This first basilica was almost immediately replaced by a second basilica ('B'), built just south of and parallel to the forum. Its massive piers of brick and stone still reveal the scale and strength of what was a more 'squat' design, as broad as it was long. Its wide nave and side aisles were lined with columns of precious green marble, whose white capitals were sculptured with fish and acanthus. The designs are similar to those in the Sancta Sophia in Istanbul, and it seems probable that artists from Constantinople shared in this project. Both buildings must have been built at about the same time.

Once again, however, catastrophe struck the Christian community at Philippi. Before the basilica was completed and dedicated, the great dome supported on its four piers collapsed and was never replaced. Only in the tenth century was a smaller church built in the basilica narthex which extended into the original nave, as can be seen today. As in basilica 'A', there was a baptistery outside the north aisle and other service rooms. To the south of the basilica are the remains of baths and latrines. To the east, at present inaccessible under excavation, is what may well have been a 'pilgrim' complex with an octagonal chapel, another baptistery, a hospice and baths, all approached by a colonnade off the Via Egnatia.

Finally, no visit to Philippi is complete without a call at one of the possible sites of Lydia's baptism 'outside the city gate by the riverside' (Acts 16:13). There is an early basilica outside the Neapolis Gate beside a small stream. A mile and a half outside the Krenides Gate there *was* a Roman arch over the Via Egnatia near the River Gangites – rather far from the city perhaps. But the most accessible and perhaps probable site, just outside the Krenides Gate itself, beside the Krenides River – a tributary of the Gangites – is a spot to which a Roman road leads from the city. The paved road is still clearly visible, lined with monuments to Roman officials and leading to the bank of the stream. Here is, today, a beautiful little Orthodox church of St Lydia and a convenient waterside baptistery, a heavenly place to recall our own baptism and renew our baptismal vows.

Scripture References:
Acts 16:11–40
        20:6
1 Thessalonians 2:1 and 2
Philippians (especially 1:1–11; 2:1–18)

19

THE VIA EGNATIA

Paul and his friends travelled from the port of Neapolis, modern Kavalla, where a stone outside the Orthodox Church of St Paul 'marks' his landing place, over the hill to Philippi (Acts 16:11, 12). Today, the Via Egnatia can be easily traced and walked for long stretches out of Kavalla suburbs. The original road was about ten feet wide and is still straight and strong. It continues over the rise to the north-west and the acropolis of Philippi is soon in sight, and one can visualise the swampy battlefields of 42 B.C. off to the left, or south-west. It runs through the centre of Philippi north-west, between the forum on the left and the acropolis and theatre on the right. Here it is constructed of long flagstones which still show the ruts of the chariot wheels.

After their miraculous deliverance, Paul and Silas continued through Amphipolis and Apollonia, behind Mount Pangaion, crossing the River Strymon at Amphipolis. Colonised by the Athenians, it was taken by Philip of Macedon, and under the Romans it was capital of the first district of Macedonia. The town was on a hill east of the river, which protected it on three sides. In the excavation of the town, a great marble lion was found, probably erected in the fourth century B.C. to commemorate the victory of Philip. The lion now stands by the roadside at the river mouth. Paul most certainly would have known the lion, which has a rather Assyrian or oriental style.

The Via Egnatia continues round the Gulf of Strymon and

Via Egnatia

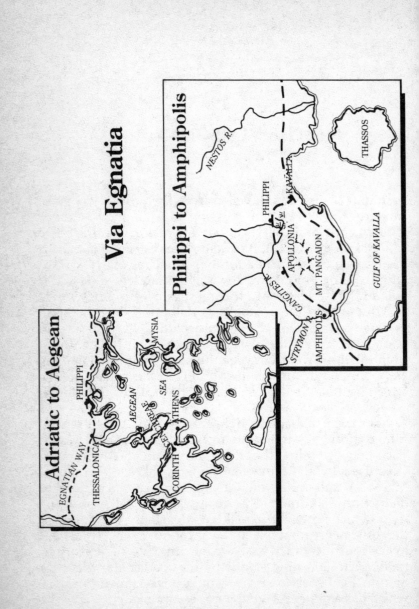

Philippi to Amphipolis

NESTOS R.

THASSOS

PHILIPPI

KAVALLA

APOLLONIA

GANGITES R.

MT. PANGAION

STRYMON R.

AMPHIPOLIS

GULF OF KAVALLA

Adriatic to Aegean

EGNATIAN WAY

PHILIPPI

THESSALONICA

MYSIA

AEGEAN SEA

CENCHREAE

ATHENS

CORINTH

south of the twelve-mile-long Lake of Volvi. There are hot sulphur springs near the modern village of Nea Apollonia, which preserves the name – if not the site – of ancient Apollonia, mentioned in Acts 17:1. There is no easily visible trace of the Via Egnatia until the centre of Thessalonica, whose modern main street axis is called 'The Via Egnatia', but the Arch of Galerius stands on the site of an earlier Arch of Augustus over the Egnatia. From Thessalonica, at the Arch of Augustus, the road forked south to Athens, but the Via Egnatia ran due west past Pella to an Adriatic coastal port also named Apollonia.

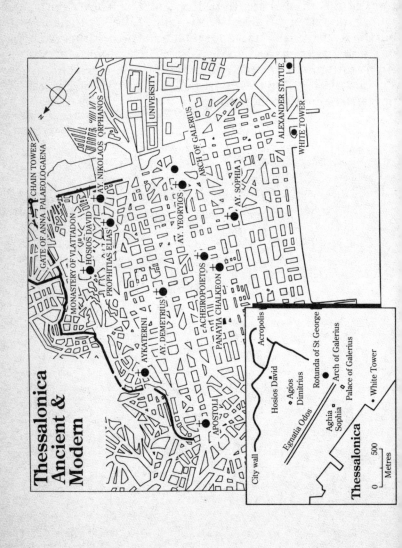

Thessalonica
Ancient & Modern

CHAIN TOWER

GATE OF ANNA PALAEOLOGAENA

AY. NIKOLAOS ORPHANOS

UNIVERSITY

MONASTERY OF VLATTADON

HOSIOS DAVID

PROPHITAS ELIAS

ARCH OF GALERIUS

AY. YEORYIOS

AY. DEMETRIUS

AYKATERINI

ACHEIROPOIETOS

PANAYIA CHALKEON

AY. SOPHIA

ALEXANDER STATUE

WHITE TOWER

APOSTOLI

Thessalonica

City wall

Acropolis

Hosios David

Agios Dimitrius

Egnatia Odos

Rotunda of St George

Arch of Galerius

Aghia Sophia

Palace of Galerius

White Tower

0   500

Metres

20

THESSALONICA

Thessalonica is at the head of the largest gulf in the Aegean. It was a thermal gulf, originally called after the local hot springs, 'The Gulf of Thermae'. The city itself was founded in 315 B.C. by one of Alexander the Great's generals, Cassander, and renamed after Cassander's wife, a half-sister of Alexander called Thessalonike. Helped by the building of the Via Egnatia and by its support of Octavius and Mark Antony before the battle of Philippi, the city prospered. It became the seat of the proconsul of the province, a free city with its own city council of five executive officers, called 'politarchs'.

The Emperor Constantine mustered his fleet off Thessalonica in A.D. 324, but it was Theodosius who made Thessalonica a metropolitan see, the seat of an archbishop – and the base of Theodosius' operations against the Goths. Here, Theodosius was himself converted to Christianity. To this period belong the imposing ramparts which dominate the city today. In the time of Justinian in the sixth century, Thessalonica became the second city of the Byzantine empire.

Nowadays, Thessalonica is a vast concrete university city, within Greece second only to Athens. The core of the city remains the fortified city of Theodosius, whose walls still run from the sea-front up to the acropolis. Within these walls was a large imperial complex of palace, circus and mausoleum, near the triple Arch of Galerius, whose central piers record the triumphs of that 'bull-necked, pale-faced pagan' emperor over the Parthians. The reliefs depict lions, elephants and camels – besides Galerius' father-in-law Diocletian and ranks of prisoners wearing the Phrygian pointed caps. Galerius succeeded Diocletian as Eastern Emperor in A.D. 292 and resided in Thessalonica.

Higher up the hill and once linked to the arch by a colonnaded street was the mausoleum of Galerius, a vast brick rotunda which was subsequently dedicated as a Christian church of St George. In Turkish times, this magnificent building was converted into a mosque, whose minaret still stands. The huge brick cylinder is made up of eight bays supporting a shallow dome. As a result of considerable earthquake damage in very recent years, the Rotunda of St George has been closed to the public for repairs, but the impressive exterior alone adds to the visitor's impression of the splendour of the Byzantine city.

Nearer the arch are the remains of the Palace of Galerius, still under excavation; while to the south-east, now partly covered by the International Fair compound, was the circus. Here, in A.D. 390, Theodosius ordered the systematic massacre of more than 7,000 citizens in punishment for the murders of his Gothic military commanders.

Thessalonica is a city of beautiful churches in the Byzantine style, if not all of the Byzantine period. Among these are those of the Mother of God, 'not made with human hands', fifth century; Holy David (not the king but a local holy man), fifth century; the cathedral basilica of St Demetrius, also fifth century (of whom more later); Holy Wisdom, eleventh century. Then there are three fourteenth-century churches: the Holy Apostles, St Catherine's and St Nicholas'.

If the visitor was limited to two, I would suggest the Holy Apostles as one of the most beautiful aesthetically and interesting archaeologically and in a quiet corner of the city. The Basilica of St Demetrius, however, is the spiritual and geographical centre of the city. Its long history, culminating in an almost total reconstruction after the great fire of 1917, is well illustrated in its crypt, chapels and mosaics.

Demetrius was a military officer under Galerius in the fourth century, but on his becoming a Christian he was arrested and held prisoner in the local baths, on the order of the emperor. At the same time, his friend and fellow officer Nestor, also recently converted to Christianity, challenged and killed an imperial gladiator. The two friends, suspected of collusion, were summarily executed, Nestor by the sword and Demetrius speared to death within the public baths.

From the fifth century, Demetrius has been venerated within a basilica on this site as the guardian of the city, the protector of its children and healer of its sick. The fine mosaics illustrate the success of his intercessions in all three capacities down the centuries. The scene of his martyrdom is preserved within the crypt.

The Byzantine city of Theodosius was enclosed within a triangle, whose base was the sea-front and whose apex was the acropolis. On the north side, the ramparts ran diagonally down the hill from the Chain Tower – passing just outside the site of the Holy Apostles Church – from where they can be seen today. On the south side, the ramparts ran straight down the hill, passing just within the Arch of Galerius, and sections of the wall remain.

In the time of St Paul, the first-century city is more likely to have been divided between the acropolis and the waterfront and linked, as in Athens, by long walls. So, the main places traditionally linked with St Paul and the primitive Church are to be found on or near the acropolis. As these are not easily found or entered, I would suggest the following in order:

1 A walk on or beside the ramparts to the Chain Tower and an orientation of the Byzantine city below.
2 The monastic chapel of the Vlattadon, whose southern 'transept' floor includes a preaching stone of St Paul. In the modern Patriarchal Institute, within the monastery grounds, the manuscripts from Mount Athos are being stored on microfilm.
3 The fifth-century chapel of Hosios David, once part of

another monastic complex, with a recently uncovered early mosaic of a beardless Christ. Presumably this dates from before the standardisation of the bearded face.

On either side of the young Christ are figures of Ezekiel and Habakkuk, both prophets famous for their mystical meditation. The Christ sits on a rainbow in glory, while at his feet are the four rivers of Paradise, with fish and subjugated pagan river-god. The apocalyptic symbols of the Evangelists decorate the corners: the lion of St Mark, the ox of St Luke, the angel of St Matthew and the eagle of St John.

4   Walk back up to the acropolis and through the gate in the walls, over a road behind the Chain Tower to a garden in which is a traditional shrine of a 'Well of St Paul'. Across the street is a modern Orthodox church of St Paul.

Even in St Paul's day, the city had a fine harbour and a rich textile industry. It included a wide span of social strata and accommodation, from waterfront slums to hillside palaces. The Greek philosopher Strabo described the city as 'Populous and easy-going, open to everything new – good and bad'. There must have been a large Jewish community, in whose synagogue Paul preached on three successive Sabbaths.

He is likely to have spent a good three months, rather than the three weeks Luke indicates, because he received money from the Christian community at Philippi, 100 miles distant. That was in the year 50 and he revisited Thessalonica in transit on his third missionary journey in c. 56. His first letter to the Church at Thessalonica is the oldest document of the New Testament, written from Corinth soon after his first visit to Thessalonica. It gives insight into his pastoral policy. He and his companions never stopped earning their keep by his old trade of tent-making. He did his pastoral visiting after a long day's work. His contacts were warm and affectionate, in great humility, but with great inner strength and intellect. He, himself, had been a Jewish convert; he knew the problems – the sense of loneliness and isolation, the loss of confidence and security. Each Church began with a single family, round which the little Christian community could gather. This provided a home for the 'family liturgy': Lydia's house at Philippi, Aquila and Priscilla's at Corinth, Jason's at Thessalonica.

It was Paul's acceptance by the Gentile or Pagan god-fearers that so infuriated the Orthodox Jews. They carried out an attack on Paul's base in Thessalonica – Jason's house. Not finding Paul, they dragged Jason before the politarchs. These, however, were of considerably higher grade than the magistrates at Philippi. When their authority was invoked, they were not impressed and released Jason on bail against a recurrence of the disturbance. But, nevertheless, Thessalonica had become too hot for Paul and he moved on, via Beroea to Athens.

In Paul's day the Via Egnatia, running as it still does, through the city centre, passed under an arch, *then* the Arch of Augustus. It is significant that Paul, passing under that arch, then turned south towards Athens, rather than continue on towards Rome. It must have involved a conscious decision to divert from his ultimate objective to reach the imperial city.

Scripture References:
Acts 17:1–14
    27:2
Philippians 4:15–17
2 Timothy 4:9 and 10
1 & 2 Thessalonians

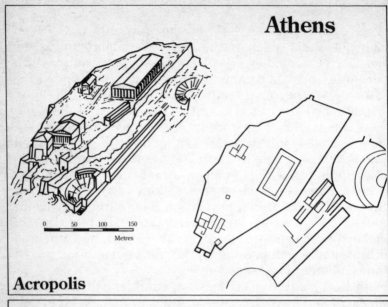

Athens

Acropolis

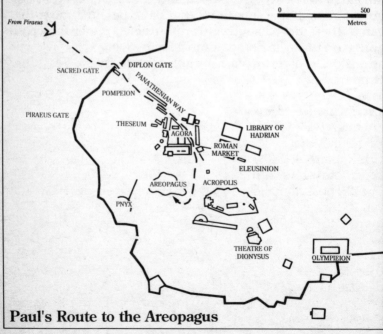

From Piraeus

SACRED GATE
DIPLON GATE

PIRAEUS GATE

POMPEION

PANATHENIAN WAY

THESEUM

AGORA

ROMAN MARKET

LIBRARY OF HADRIAN

ELEUSINION

AREOPAGUS

ACROPOLIS

PNYX

THEATRE OF DIONYSUS

OLYMPIEION

0   500
Metres

Paul's Route to the Areopagus

21

PAUL IN ATHENS

Some of what follows is based on the 'travel diaries' of two near-contemporaries – *viz*: 'The Life of Apollonius of Tyana' and 'The Diary of Pausanias'. Both landed at Piraeus – one of the many harbours of Athens. The legendary kings sailed from Phaleron, five miles from the city centre. A Christian basilica, traditionally linked with Paul, is at Glyphada. But the largest harbour is at Piraeus (actually three harbours in one). Themistocles the statesman/general who created the Athenian navy chose Piraeus as the port of Athens. He built walls to fortify the harbour. He linked it to the city by 'long' walls, between which (on the axis of the modern road) the ancient highway ran to the Diplon Gate. Along this highway both Apollonius and Pausanias entered the city, so probably Paul did too.

Outside the city at this point was a quarter occupied by potters and metal workers, also an extensive cemetery. At this point, too, the road from Plato's Academy also entered the city by the Sacred Gate, and the Double (or Diplon) Gate built in 330 B.C. From here, the Dromos (literally *the* Road) ran into the city, across the Inner Kerameikos (Ceramics) quarter to the agora. From the agora, the Panathenaic (foot) Way led to the base of the acropolis.

The agora was the centre of the public and business life of the city. Here people met every day to hear the news and discuss all kinds of subjects. The agora was full of temples, government buildings, shops, offices and altars. Endless statues, stoas and colonnades protected folk from the sun and rain. (Detailed plans of both the agora and acropolis are to be found on p. 106.) The Sacred Way runs diagonally across the agora – the civic centre – and climbs up through the Propylaea on to the acropolis – the religious centre.

Below the acropolis and overlooking the agora is the Areopagus, literally Mars Hill.

Pausanias describes this barren rock as a place of trial – with a 'Stone of Outrage' and a 'Stone of Ruthlessness' on which stood the defendants and prosecutors, during legal proceedings. He speaks of a nearby sanctuary of the Furies, who avenged the crime of murder. He says that persons acquitted in trials here on the hill, went to the sanctuary to offer sacrifice in thanksgiving.

The court that met here on the rock was also called the Areopagus, or the Council of the Areopagus. Although it dealt in early days with capital crime, by the time of Paul it dealt with religious affairs as well. The usual expression for appearing before this tribunal was: 'to go up into Areopagus', the traditional meeting place of the court. However, a fourth-century inscription, found in the Stoa of Attalus, mentions an entrance to the Areopagus within the Bouleterion. Demosthenes also describes the Areopagus sitting in the Royal Stoa. So, the court must – on occasion (perhaps wet weather) – have met down in the agora.

ACTS 17:16–34

Paul's first impression is of the city 'full of idols'. Livy too describes: 'statues of gods and men – notable for every material and artistry'. Paul – true to form – began in the synagogue, then in the market place with all and sundry who were prepared to listen. Some Epicurean and Stoic philosophers met him and took him to the Areopagus – most likely up to this rock.

Here, Paul began with a compliment, remarking on how very religious the Athenians were, saying he had even seen an altar to an *unknown* god!

Pausanias exactly parallels this, saying, 'Athenians are conspicuous not only for their humanity, but also for their devotion to religion.' He even mentions 'altars of the gods named UNKNOWN'. Apollonius, too, mentions altars to unknown gods.

Paul's quotation, 'For we are indeed his offspring' is a quotation from 'Phenomena' by Aratus, a third-century B.C. poet from Paul's native Cilicia. The works of Aratus must have been studied with pride in the schools of Tarsus and came naturally from the lips of Paul.

In the climax of his address, Paul refers to the Resurrection. He had first passed through that vast cemetery outside the Diplon Gate. Perhaps he remembered the Eumenides of Aeschylus (about the Areopagus) in which Apollo says: 'Whenever the dust of the earth drinks up the blood of a man who has died, there is *no* resurrection.'

Christian faith was already being applied even to the pagan concept of burial grounds. The Greek word *koimeterion* meant both dormitory *and* burial place. Paul soon used the figure of 'sleep' to the Thessalonians: 'We would not have you ignorant, brethren, concerning those who are asleep, that you may not grieve as others do, who have no hope' (1 Thess. 4:13).

Several centuries later, St John Chrysostom, on the word 'cemetery', said: 'Before the coming of Christ, death was called death. Now, it's called sleep. The place where we bury our loved ones is called a "koimeterion", or dormitory.'

Among those who believed Paul, was a woman called Damaris (who John Chrysostom wrote was the wife of Dionysius!) and also Dionysius, one of the council, who, according to later sources, became head of the Church of Athens.

Aristides, an Athenian philosopher, very aware of both Paul and Dionysius, was a powerful Christian apologist. Athenagoras, also a second-century Athenian philosopher, wrote a powerful and sublime treatise on the Resurrection.

Both reflected on the apostle's teaching, completing what
Paul began on this rock of Mars Hill.

Scripture References:
Acts 17:15–34
1 Thessalonians 3:1 and 2

22

CORINTH

It was at Corinth, during his *second* journey, that Paul conducted a mission (from perhaps the winter of the years 49 and 50 to the summer of the year 51), described by Luke in Acts 18:1–18. Later, during his third journey, he conducted a considerable correspondence with the Christian community at Corinth, writing from Ephesus between the years 54 and 57, during which time he also paid a brief visit to Corinth. Although Paul built up a flourishing Christian congregation at Corinth, which he left in the care of Apollos, a learned Alexandrian Jewish convert, the Corinthian Church played a relatively small part in the later history of the Christian Church in the eastern Mediterranean.

Corinth was an important and wealthy city astride the Isthmus of Corinth and controlling the ports on either side, Lechaeum on the west, Cenchreae on the east. Corinth was the capital of the Roman province of Achaia, the southern part of Greece, and the seat of the Roman proconsul. It was a city of great commerce, wealth, and squalor, renowned for its culture and notorious for its immorality. Lying on the great trade-route between Rome and the east, with a very mixed commercial and cosmopolitan community, Corinth was of strategic importance in the spreading of Christianity throughout the eastern Mediterranean.

Travellers could avoid the dangerous voyage round the Peloponnese by crossing the Isthmus of Corinth from harbour to harbour. The international character of the city

Corinth

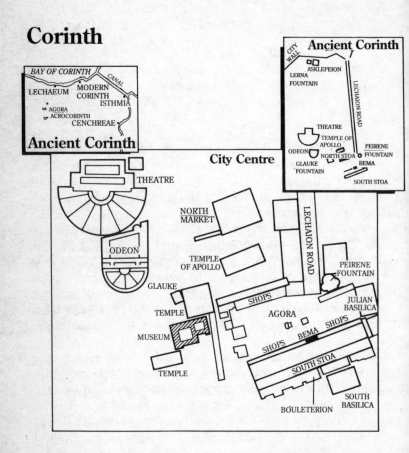

Ancient Corinth

BAY OF CORINTH

CANAL

LECHAEUM

MODERN
CORINTH

ISTHMIA

AGORA

ACROCORINTH

CENCHREAE

Ancient Corinth

CITY
WALL

ASKLEPEION

LERNA
FOUNTAIN

LECHAION ROAD

THEATRE

TEMPLE OF
APOLLO

ODEON

NORTH STOA

PEIRENE
FOUNTAIN

GLAUKE
FOUNTAIN

BEMA

SOUTH STOA

City Centre

THEATRE

NORTH
MARKET

LECHAION ROAD

ODEON

TEMPLE
OF APOLLO

PEIRENE
FOUNTAIN

GLAUKE

SHOPS

JULIAN
BASILICA

TEMPLE

AGORA

MUSEUM

BEMA

SHOPS

SHOPS

TEMPLE

SOUTH STOA

BOULETERION

SOUTH
BASILICA

fostered the development of a variety of cults from as far away as Egypt and Phoenicia. The chief shrine, however, was the temple of the Greek goddess of love – Aphrodite – although the cult was debased by foreign influences. The priestess-prostitutes of Aphrodite at Corinth are said to have numbered one thousand.

Paul came to Corinth after his highly unsuccessful visit to Athens. Filled with disappointment, in fear and trembling, he made his way over the Isthmus to the city in the winter of 49–50. There he remained for eighteen months, living and working as a tentmaker with Aquila and his wife Priscilla, Jews expelled from Rome by the edict of Claudius in the year 49. On the arrival of Timothy and Silas, they taught both Jews and Greeks in the synagogue and then in a private house. As a result, a large Church was formed at Corinth, mostly from the poor and slave classes. During this time Paul, receiving Timothy's report from Thessalonica, sent his first letter to that Church about the second coming of Jesus. Following further reports he sent his second letter, warning the Thessalonians not to use the teaching of justification by faith as an excuse for lawlessness, but to persevere in faith and well-doing. In both these letters, Paul's intensity and affection are conveyed and reveal the power of his personality.

With the arrival of a new proconsul of Achaia, called Gallio, in the year 51, certain members of the Jewish community of Corinth accused Paul of teaching religion 'contrary to the Law'. Gallio refused to adjudicate, but the time had come for Paul and his party to move on. Sailing from Cenchreae, the eastern harbour of Corinth, he reached Ephesus, on the west coast of Asia Minor. After a brief preliminary visit to the synagogue and promising to return on his next journey, Paul sailed for Caesarea, where he greeted the Christian Church on his way north by road to Antioch. This second journey of 2,800 miles must have taken three years, the greater part of which was spent at Corinth.

The following is one of many theories of the circum-

stances of Paul's correspondence with Corinth as suggested by Archbishop Wand.

During his time in Ephesus, Paul had heard news from
Corinth that made it necessary for him to write to warn that
Christian community against associating with immoral persons. He then probably wrote what is now to be found in 2
Corinthians 6:14–7:1. Shortly afterwards, he received an
official letter from the Corinthian Church asking advice on
specific matters, such as the celebration of the Eucharist
and the doctrine of the Resurrection. Paul had also heard
that party spirit prevailed in that community and that a
particularly grave case of immorality had arisen within the
Church. Paul dealt with these questions in a letter now
known to us as 1 Corinthians, which he sent by sea, while
Timothy took the land route to deal with the situation in
person. Neither the letter nor Timothy's visit achieved the
desired effect, and Paul himself sailed for Corinth. Even he
was not able to secure a reform within the Corinthian
Christian community and, after being grossly insulted, he
sailed back to Ephesus. From there, he wrote a 'severe
letter', his third, part of which is probably to be found in 2
Corinthians chapters 10–13, which was carried by Titus, an
older and more experienced man than Timothy. This letter
demanded a proper respect both for Christian morality and
for Paul, as founder of the Church in Corinth.

When Paul finally closed his ministry at Ephesus, he
travelled north overland to Troas, whence he sailed once
again for Macedonia to visit Philippi, Thessalonica, and
Beroea. Somewhere en route he met Titus, who at last
brought him the good news that the Corinthian Church
was ready to conform, and that they had already by a
majority vote censured the person who had insulted Paul.
Paul immediately wrote his fourth letter, to be found in 2
Corinthians chapters 1–9. In this last letter, he forgave his
antagonist, closed the controversy, and arranged for a
collection to be taken for the poor at Jerusalem. Paul seems
to have travelled overland to Corinth, where he spent the
winter months, in which time he wrote his letter to the

Christian Church in Rome, to prepare them for his coming and to secure their support for a journey to Spain.

Paul's plan to sail directly from Corinth to Jerusalem, taking his poor-relief collection, was thwarted by some threat of ambush. Consequently he returned overland to Macedonia.

Today, the Corinthian Canal, conceived by Nero, but not completed until 1893, joins the Aegean and Ionian Seas. The city of Paul's day was magnificent. Imperial favour and local wealth combined to build a circuit of six miles of walls around a lavish display of marble public buildings. The Lechaeum road on which Paul would have approached the city was twenty-five feet wide and flanked by sidewalks or pavements. Within the city raised promenades were lined with colonnades of shops on both sides. In the centre of the city, the Temple of Apollo was the only building to survive a cruel siege in 146 B.C. Seven of its original thirty-eight massive columns are still standing – six feet in diameter. At the entrance to the agora (south of the temple) is the famous Fountain of Peirene. The agora (or market) was divided by a rostrum (or bema) flanked by lines of shops. This rostrum or pulpit was the focus of the agora, from which speakers could address the crowds. Here, perhaps, Paul was

brought before the governor Gallio. We know from an inscription that Gallio became governor of Achaia in the year 51 to 52. The museum at Ancient Corinth includes evidence of the Corinthian Jewish community – including several 'menora' and one stone with the words, 'The Synagogue of the Hebrews'.

On his departure, Paul sailed from the eastern harbour Cenchreae for Ephesus.

Scripture References:
Acts 18:1–18
     19:1
1 & 2 Corinthians (especially 1, 2 and 13)

Part Five:

THIRD MISSIONARY JOURNEY

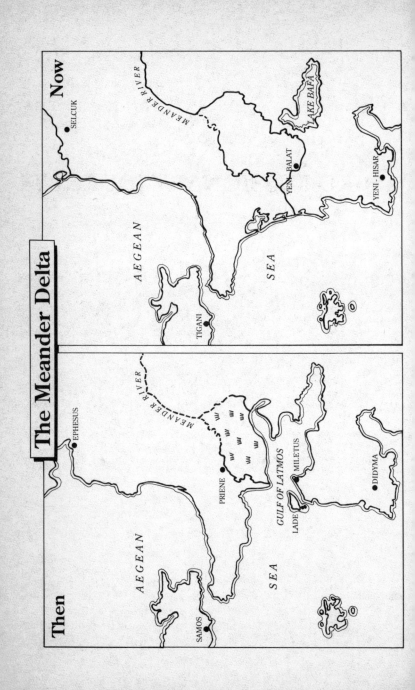

The Meander Delta

Then

AEGEAN

SEA

SAMOS

EPHESUS

MEANDER RIVER

PRIENE

GULF OF LATMOS

LADE

MILETUS

DIDYMA

Now

AEGEAN

SEA

SELCUK

MEANDER RIVER

YENI-BALAT

LAKE BAFA

YENI-HISAR

TIGANI

23

THE CITY OF EPHESUS: LINKS WITH ST JOHN, ST PAUL AND THE VIRGIN MARY

The ancient city of Ephesus underwent three *main periods of occupation*: from its foundation in c. 980 B.C. to its conquest by the Lydian King Croesus in 560 B.C., from this Lydian occupation to its conquest by Lysimachus, one of the successors of Alexander, and finally from 290 B.C. onwards.

1 During the *Archaic* period, the city stood at the mouth of the River Cayster on the coast between Smyrna (Izmir) and Miletus, at the crossroads of the Ionian, Lydian (N) and Carian (S) territories. During the Ionian Renaissance, it produced philosophers and poets.

2 During the *Lydian* period Croesus built the Temple of Artemis known to St Paul and St John, on the site of an earlier shrine. The temple was burned down, on the very night that Alexander was born in 354 B.C. When, twenty years later, Alexander offered to rebuild the temple, the Ephesians declined his offer and rebuilt it themselves at great sacrifice and with great magnificence.

3 During the *Greco-Roman* period, on the death of Alexander's successor Lysimachus in 281 B.C., Ephesus came under the control of the Seleucids, who were in turn defeated by the Romans at the battle of Magnesia in 189 B.C. At first a Roman vassal to Pergamum, Ephesus grew in importance through the attentions of successive

Ephesus
Greco-Roman City   Byzantine Basilicas

1. MAGNESIA GATE
2. PUBLIC MARKET
3. TEMPLE OF DOMITIAN
4. BATHS
5. LITTLE THEATRE
6. CITY HALL
7. **TRAJAN'S FOUNTAIN**
8. THE WAY OF CURETES
9. PALACES
10. TEMPLE OF HADRIAN
11. LIBRARY OF CELSIUS
12. HOUSES
13. MARKET PLACE
14. THEATRE
15. THEATRE GYMNASIUM
16. ARCADIAN WAY
17. HARBOUR BATHS
18. ANCIENT HARBOUR
19. DOUBLE CHURCH
20. GYMNASIUM OF VEDIUS
21. STADIUM
22. SITE OF TEMPLE OF ARTEMIS
23. MOSQUE OF ISSA BEY
24. BASILICA OF ST.JOHN
25. THE CASTLE CITADEL
26. HELLENISTIC RAMPARTS
27. BYZANTINE RAMPARTS
28. EASTERN GYMNASIUM

•••••• Possible pilgrim route through city

emperors, until in the time of Hadrian in A.D. 125, the city was made the imperial capital of Asia. St Paul and St John lived in the city at the height of its political importance and pagan notoriety. In the New Testament period, Ephesus was the fourth greatest city in the world, after Rome, Alexandria and Antioch, with a population of a quarter of a million.

Owing to the lack of tides in the Mediterranean to scour the sediment deposited in river-mouth harbours, the coastline of Asia Minor has receded some six miles in 2,000 years. As early as 499 B.C. the Greeks were not able to land at the river-mouth. The Archaic period city must have surrounded the present site of the ancient Temple of Artemis. When the harbour silted up, the city was moved a mile and a half towards the sea and a Sacred Way linked city and sanctuary. Pliny the Elder, Roman historian, describes how the waters of the harbour lapped the end of the Arcadian Way. In A.D. 129, the Emperor Hadrian provided for the dredging of the harbour and the diversion of the river course in order to preserve the port. In the sixth century, the city was moved back to the acropolis of the Archaic period, overlooking the site of the Temple of Artemis – where it was more easily defensible than on the low marshland by the river. Little stands on the acropolis today but the ruins of the magnificent Byzantine Basilica of St John.

The Greco-Roman city remains today – a magnificent complex of temples, libraries, baths, gymnasia and theatres, linked by a splendid marble street which runs from the Magnesia Gate to the Roman agora or market place. Here the riotous silversmiths had their shops and the Great Theatre virtually climbed the hill beyond the agora. Here in the theatre 24,000 shouting Ephesians protested against Paul's ministry in Ephesus. The huge theatre made a magnificent focal point for all who landed in the harbour and surveyed the city up the vista of the Arcadian Way. As one approaches by road from the west today, the view must very much resemble that from ships arriving up the river into the harbour, at the time of St Paul. Through avenues of statues and columns, the many public buildings glistening white in the sunshine extended up the hillsides as far as the city walls.

Here, Paul spent the first three months of his ministry teaching in the synagogue, after going 'from place to place through the region of Galatia and Phrygia' strengthening all the disciples from his previous two missionary journeys. When his break with the Jewish community occurred, he moved to the lecture-room of a Gentile called Tyrannus. There he taught daily among both Jews and Greeks for a period of two whole years (55–57) in the siesta hours of noon to four in the afternoon, when it was too hot for normal student studies. Remarkable progress followed this systematic instruction, which was accompanied also by Paul's ministry of healing. Both Jews and Greeks came to respect the name of Jesus, rather than the magical arts of Diana or Artemis of the Ephesians. Paul despatched teachers to Colossae and Macedonia. At this time also, the seven churches (or parishes) of Asia, mentioned by St John in the Revelation on Patmos, were founded.

When Paul closed his ministry at Ephesus, he travelled north overland to Troas, crossed into Macedonia, visited his Greek congregations and made his way down to Corinth for the winter months of the year 57–58. In the spring, on his way back to Jerusalem for Pentecost, Paul's ship did not put in to Ephesus – and so he called the Elders of Ephesus to meet him at Miletus.

The link between St John and Mary, the mother of Jesus, with Ephesus was established by the fifth century. You will remember the words from the cross of Jesus: 'Woman behold thy son, Son behold thy mother' and how St John took the mother of Jesus 'away to his own home'. The Ephesian theory is that, following the dispersal of the apostles from Jerusalem, John took Mary to Ephesus. Paul's failure to mention either John or Mary's presence may be compared with the fact that he made no mention of Peter's mission to Rome, although Peter died there, before Paul did.

In the fifth century, Pope Celestine referred to Ephesus as the home of Mary and of John. Hippolytus of Thebes in the seventh century mentioned that Mary had lived for eleven years at Ephesus before her death. This tradition survived the Muslim occupation of Ephesus in 1090 and thrived among the scattered Christian community in the surrounding villages. Since the year 1914, a small shrine in the Byzantine style, rather south of the present ruins of Ephesus, has been a place of Latin pilgrimage and devotion accepted by Papal authority as symbolising the house of Mary in Ephesus.

Perhaps the most significant factor is that the Third Great Ecumenical Council, held at Ephesus in the year 431, established the Virgin Mary in Christian doctrine, as *theotokos*, the 'mother of God'. The council met in the huge double basilica still to be seen and 800 feet long, which was itself dedicated to Mary.

Our visit to Ephesus is designed to include the Greco-Roman city, the museum, the Church of St John, the Double Church of St Mary and the traditional house of Mary. Virtually nothing is to be seen of the Temple of Artemis – once one of the Seven Wonders of the Ancient World. We shall, however, hear more of this in connection with our visit to Patmos and with the Revelations or visions of perhaps another and later John.

The drawing on the previous page shows a notice carved in the pavement of the Marble Street outside the commercial agora, showing the way to the brothel on the opposite side of the road. It includes the notice board, the man's footstep, the lady's face, the heart for love, and the bag of money.

Scripture References:
John 19:25–27
Acts 18:18–28
       19:1–20:1
       20:16 and 17
1 Timothy 1:3
2 Timothy 1:18
          4:12
Revelation 1:11
          2:1–7
Ephesians (especially 1 and 6)

24

PRIENE, CITY OF ALEXANDER

This little city of Alexander is one of the most attractive and intimate of the ancient sites on the west coast. It is essentially a small city of small buildings, whose ruins are well-preserved and excavated. It is a Greek city and its public buildings, streets and houses are those of the days of Alexander.

There was an earlier city founded during the Ionian migration, a member of the Ionian League, whose site has never been found, but no doubt lies buried beneath the mud of the Meander. There remain no inscriptions and few records of the ancient Priene, and just one single coin!

In the Ionian age, the site of the Panionium – the regional Olympic Games – was within the territory of Priene and largely staffed by Prienians. And in those days, the harbour and coastline were at the foot of the hill on which the new town of Alexander was begun in 334 B.C.

On Alexander's personal visit and initiative the population of the ancient harbour site, by then no longer on the coastline, was transferred to the new town. Alexander undertook the cost of building a Temple of Athena in return for the privilege of making the dedication – as he had done already at Ephesus. Whereas the Ephesians had rejected his offer, the Prienians were less proud and accepted. The architect was a Carian, called Pytheos, who wrote a book taking this Atheneum at Priene as a model of temple construction. This book survived as a text-book into Roman times.

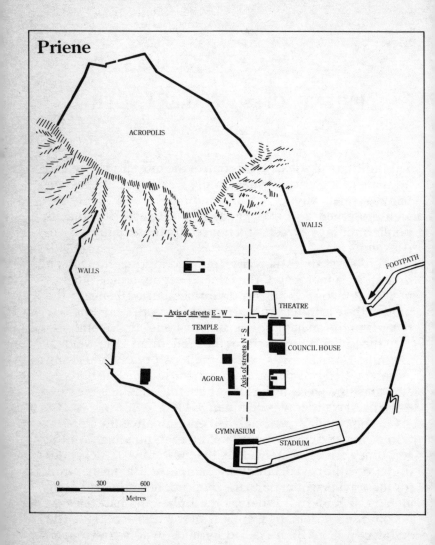

Priene

ACROPOLIS

WALLS

WALLS

FOOTPATH

Axis of streets E - W

TEMPLE

THEATRE

Axis of streets N - S

COUNCIL HOUSE

AGORA

GYMNASIUM

STADIUM

0   300   600
Metres

An open courtyard, half the area of the temple building, leads up steps into a colonnade or cloister surrounding the temple proper. The worshipper continued through another pair of columns into the antechamber and up another set of steps through a doorway into the main room, at the back and centre of which was the cult statue. Behind, but connected with the main room, was a rear chamber often used as a treasury. Ancient temples were not used for congregational services. They were thought of as houses for the god to which they were dedicated, and entered by the priests only on special occasions, while the people remained outside in the courtyard.

Another attractive and better-preserved building is the council house. This was a tiny rectangular theatre, with rows of seats on three sides. On the fourth side are stone benches for the presiding officials, flanked by two doors. In the centre is a decorated altar for the sacrifices with which every public assembly began. The city council (or boule), the chief instrument of government, met here to prepare measures for submission to the general assembly. As the council chamber could seat 640 persons, it could probably seat the whole assembly also. If there was an assembly of 600 enfranchised members, that would presuppose a total city population of 3,000 persons.

The theatre is an excellent example of a Hellenistic theatre, with about ten rows of seats excavated. The front row consists of five marble thrones for VIPs or (as in Athens) for priests. The 'royal box' is in the middle of the fifth row. An altar to Dionysus in the middle of the front row was used for sacrifice before each performance. Peculiar to this theatre at Priene is a water clock at the west corner of the orchestra, but only its base remains.

The stadium, some 200 yards (a stade) long and 20 yards wide, runs across the southernmost section of the city within the walls. The starting-point is at the west end, once a row of ten columns, of which the bases only remain. A simple starting-gate was probably used on each pillar. Events contested in the stadium were foot-races, wrestling, boxing, the pancration (test of strength) and the pentathlon (a competition made up of five different sports). Horse and chariot races were held in the hippodrome.

Finally, the main feature of the city is undoubtedly its site. It stands on sloping ground at the southern foot of a great cliff, on the top of which must have been the acropolis. Within this fortress was a permanent garrison, whose commandant was forbidden to leave it for his four-month term of office. The city, far below, was dominated by the Temple of Athena and sloped down to the edge of the plateau. At the foot of the plateau on the east side is the site of the ancient harbour on the level of the modern road. The city walls encircle the plateau, with three gates, and climb the cliff face to the acropolis.

EPHESUS

tre, Arcadian Way and Harbour beyond

e of Artemis in Seljuk Museum

Library of Celsius from Scholastica's Baths

Hadrian's temple on Curetes Street

PRIENE

Model Temple of Athena under the Acropolis

Council Chamber with square seating plan

above: Medusa head with snake hair

ve: Temple of Apollo, sanctuary of the oriental oracle

maid motif on column base   Detail from a frieze of griffins

MILETUS

Above: Theatre looking towards Baths of Faustina and thirteenth-century mosque

Below: Lion harbour quayside installations and baths

Inset below: One of two lions who still span the silted-up harbour

Petrified cascades
and basins formed
by a series of
lime-charged
springs

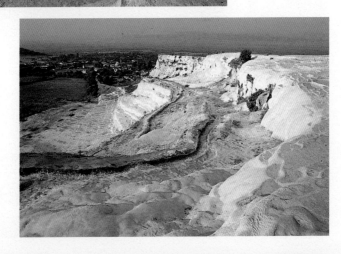

HIERAPOLIS

Left: Roman baths converted and consecrated as a Byzantine church

Above: 'Chi Ro' symbol on the keystones of the arches

Tumulus, house, and sarcophagus burials in the necropolis

Mosaic of St Paul in narthex of St Saviour in Chora

Sophia, built by Justinian, converted to a
sque, now a museum

us and John the Baptist in south gallery of Sa Sophia

PATMOS

Mosaic of builder and his monastery, on the site of a penal settlement

View of St John the Divine looking to his precious parishes on the mainland

Interior of the Orthodox Monastery of St John today

25

DIDYMA, SANCTUARY OF APOLLO

The Temple of Apollo at Didyma was the third largest building in the Hellenistic world. Third only to the Temple of Artemis at Ephesus, and the Temple of Hera on the island of Samos. I had worked out that the area of the Artemision (temple of Artemis at Ephesus) equalled that of St Paul's Cathedral. The difference in size between that and the Temple of Didyma was 3.3 feet in length and thirteen feet in width, with a total of only five columns fewer, but five feet higher at Didyma.

We have been considering Priene, the city of Alexander, very much a single period site, but the history of Apollo's sanctuary at Didyma extends from the eighth century B.C. to the fifth century B.C. and it was only finally abandoned in the fifteenth century A.D.

Another point of comparison is the sanctuary at Delphi – north-west of Athens. Both sanctuaries became places of pilgrimage for those who wished to consult the mysterious and prophetic oracle, who gave advice through the sacred priestesses, often in a state of drugged coma, but whose prophesies were sufficiently ambiguous or nebulous to cover all eventualities. So, these sanctuaries developed into international diplomatic centres, to which even heads of state made pilgrimage to seek advice. Among these were Pharaoh Necho, c. 600 B.C. (who killed good King Josiah at Megiddo) and King Croesus of Lydia, c. 550 B.C.

The Archaic sanctuary at Didyma was built in the late eighth century B.C. – a sacred enclosure surrounding a well,

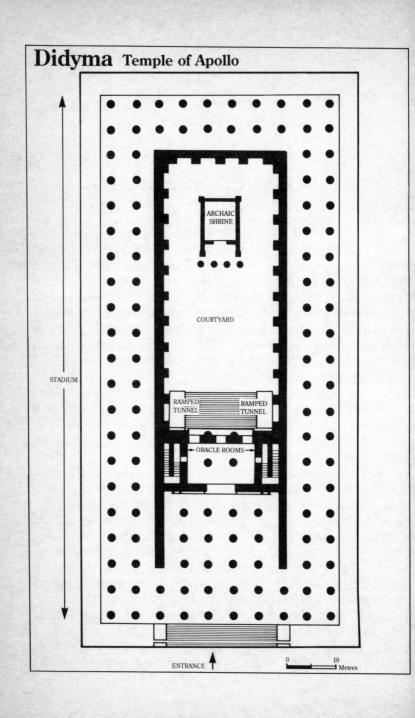

Didyma Temple of Apollo

ARCHAIC SHRINE

COURTYARD

RAMPED TUNNEL

RAMPED TUNNEL

ORACLE ROOMS

STADIUM

ENTRANCE

0   10
Metres

an altar and a laurel tree. The first temple was built in 550 B.C., enclosing a roofed shrine within a colossal temple structure open to the air. This was destroyed by the Persians in 494 B.C. when they suppressed the Ionian revolt.

On Alexander's liberation of Ionia, Miletus – the neighbouring city – rebuilt the sanctuary at Didyma on the same design, but on an even larger scale in c. 330 B.C. A life-size head of Alexander has been discovered recently. One of the architects of the Artemision was engaged to design the sanctuary at Didyma.

Whilst virtually nothing survives of the Temple of Artemis, the remains at Didyma are well-preserved and give a striking impression of what the Artemision may have looked like.

Successive Roman emperors took an interest in the sanctuary. Trajan and Hadrian were made honorary chief priests of the shrine. Trajan repaired the Sacred Way from Miletus to Didyma – cutting down hills and filling in valleys over a distance of ten miles. Although the sanctuary was sacked by the Goths in 262 B.C., it continued to function and the oracle advised Diocletian in c. A.D. 300 to continue his persecution of the Christians. But, by the fourth century, there were Christian shrines within the sanctuary, and in the fifth century a Christian basilica at the site. Earthquake and fire caused Didyma to be abandoned by the fifteenth century. The sanctuary has been well excavated by the Royal Prussian Museum – and more recently by the German Archaeological Institute in Istanbul. Some fine sculpture is still visible on site, notably a Medusa head and a marble lion.

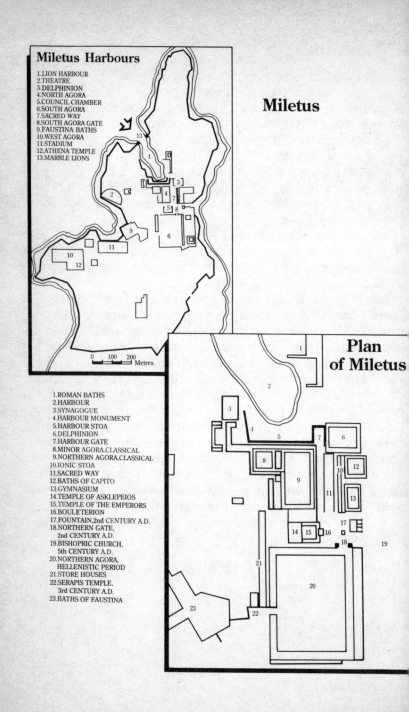

Miletus Harbours

1. LION HARBOUR
2. THEATRE
3. DELPHINION
4. NORTH AGORA
5. COUNCIL CHAMBER
6. SOUTH AGORA
7. SACRED WAY
8. SOUTH AGORA GATE
9. FAUSTINA BATHS
10. WEST AGORA
11. STADIUM
12. ATHENA TEMPLE
13. MARBLE LIONS

Miletus

0   100   200
Metres

1. ROMAN BATHS
2. HARBOUR
3. SYNAGOGUE
4. HARBOUR MONUMENT
5. HARBOUR STOA
6. DELPHINION
7. HARBOUR GATE
8. MINOR AGORA,CLASSICAL
9. NORTHERN AGORA,CLASSICAL
10. IONIC STOA
11. SACRED WAY
12. BATHS OF CAPITO
13. GYMNASIUM
14. TEMPLE OF ASKLEPEIOS
15. TEMPLE OF THE EMPERORS
16. BOULETERION
17. FOUNTAIN,2nd CENTURY A.D.
18. NORTHERN GATE,
    2nd CENTURY A.D.
19. BISHOPRIC CHURCH,
    5th CENTURY A.D.
20. NORTHERN AGORA,
    HELLENISTIC PERIOD
21. STORE HOUSES
22. SERAPIS TEMPLE,
    3rd CENTURY A.D.
23. BATHS OF FAUSTINA

Plan of Miletus

26

MILETUS, SCENE OF PAUL'S HARBOUR FAREWELL

At the time of St Paul, this one-time Ionian city stood on the site of a peninsula facing north into the Gulf of Patmos. Into the north flowed the Meander River, depositing silt so fast that the gulf was filled in and Miletus was no longer on the coastline by the fourth century. The rate of the recession of the coastline and build-up of soil was twenty feet a year, or one-third of a mile each century and Miletus is now at least five miles from the present coastline. The city once boasted four harbours: the theatre faced out on to the oldest, and the main one – called the Lion Harbour – lay 200 yards behind and to the north of the theatre. The Lion Harbour was flanked by two marble lions, was nearly a quarter of a mile long and could be closed by chains across its mouth.

The city was successively occupied by Minoans (from Crete) Mycenaeans (from the Peloponnese) and a constant stream of refugees from the Greek mainland fleeing before the Dorian invasion from the north. The city reached its greatest glory in the sixth century B.C. when its philosophers contributed to the Greek Renaissance and it colonised no less than ninety cities round the Black Sea. Little remains from this halcyon period as Miletus supported the Ionian revolt against the Persians in 499 B.C. and the Persians revenged themselves by virtually destroying both Miletus and its nearby sanctuary at Didyma. Miletus, with a population of nearly 100,000, had provided eighty triremes (sizeable ships of war) against the Persians.

Although the city was rebuilt by Hippodamus, a famous city-planner and native of Miletus, it never recovered its former glory. In the second century A.D. the emperors Trajan, Hadrian and Marcus Aurelius gave their imperial encouragement and financial support. The Sacred Way from Miletus to the sanctuary at Didyma was reconstructed on a grand scale, at the orders of Trajan. The baths, now to be seen below the theatre, were built and dedicated to the Empress Faustina, wife of Marcus Aurelius.

Among the public buildings are three agoras (market places), all from the Hellenistic period; the largest of these covered an area of eight acres and was the biggest of all Greek markets. Its eastern hall or cloister was a whole stade (200 yards) in length. The market accommodated seventy-eight stores, each of three rooms in size. Miletus was famous for its carpets, furniture and woollen textiles. A third-century price-list puts the value of dyed purple wool of the best quality at between 10 and 12,000 denarii (Roman pence) a pound.

The council chamber, which at Priene could seat 640 persons, at Miletus could accommodate 1,500. The great stadium, below the theatre, could seat 15,000, as could the theatre also. On the stage of the theatre are some fine gladiator carvings, one with a bear, another with an ibex.

The columns in the front centre remain from the canopy erected for the visit of the Empress Faustina in A.D. 164. In the fifth row of the theatre is an inscription which has been translated: 'the place of the Jews, who are also called God-fearing'. There must have been a considerable Jewish population, in Roman times, as there was a sizeable synagogue adjoining the Lion Harbour. The design of this was similar to that at Capernaum, of approximately the same date. Also adjoining the Lion Harbour was a temple of Apollo Delphinios – the Apollo of the Dolphin (the creature known as a protector and guide of seamen) – a suitable deity for a maritime community.

St Paul, returning to Jerusalem from his third missionary journey, travelled on a ship that did not call at Ephesus, but *did* put into Miletus and, doubtless, Paul came ashore at the Lion Harbour. From Miletus he sent for the Elders of Ephesus to meet him there; his touching farewell is beautifully related by St Luke in Acts 20. His last known letter (2 Tim.) mentions that he left a sick disciple, Trophimus, at Miletus – which might imply that he did make yet another visit to Miletus, before his fateful and final encounter with Alexander the coppersmith further up the coast at Troas.

Scripture References:
Acts 20:15–38
2 Timothy 4:20

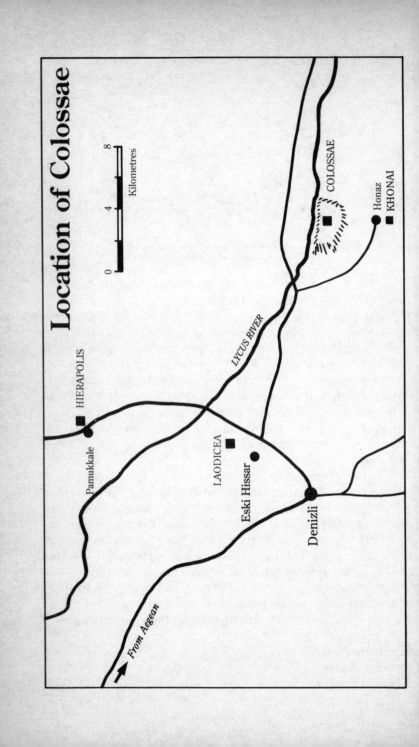

Location of Colossae

27

COLOSSAE

Once a city with an imposing name, but now a forgotten hamlet, Colossae is ten miles east of Laodicea and six miles south of Hierapolis. There is no record that St Paul personally visited Colossae, but during his long stay at Ephesus he converted Epaphras, a citizen of Colossae. Later in prison, probably at Rome, he converted the runaway slave and sent him back to his master Philemon of Colossae. Paul sent Onesimus the slave back with probably both the personal letter to Philemon and also the open letter to the Church of Colossae.

Colossae, like Laodicea and Hierapolis, lies on the main road from Ephesus to Syria, and is the earliest of the three cities. All three lie in the fertile valley of the Lycus, a tributary of the wandering Meander River – flowing west to the coast at Miletus. In the fifth century B.C. Xerxes passed through Colossae. Herodotus described it as a 'great city' strategically placed on the great highway through the interior, famous for her wool and purple dye industry. About 400 B.C., Xenophon spoke of the city as 'large and prosperous'. Pliny the Elder said it was one of the most famous in all Phrygia. The establishing of Laodicea in the third century B.C. by Antiochus II, the Seleucid King of Syria, led to the eclipse and decline of Colossae. After a brief Byzantine revival, the site was abandoned in the eighth and ninth centuries A.D. It appears to have been just a small town in the time of St Paul. The mound has never been excavated, though the acropolis and theatre are still to be seen and a few inscriptions have been found.

In his letter to the Colossians, St Paul sent his affectionate greetings and encouragement to the Christian community at Laodicea – also perhaps converted by Epaphras of Colossae. At the close of his letter, St Paul writes: 'When this letter is read among you, have it read also in the Church of the Laodiceans; and see that you read also the letter from Laodicea.' No letter to the Laodiceans has survived within the New Testament and the letter to the Ephesians may supply the clue. At least three early manuscripts omit the title or address 'to the Ephesians'. It was a common custom for congregations to exchange and read each other's letters from the apostles. It may well be that the letter to the Ephesians was a circular letter, of which as many as six copies were carried by the courier, Tychicus, on his round of the Churches in Asia. Perhaps it was he who filled in the addresses, but left at least one copy blank.

The tel or *hujuk* of Colossae is to be found some two miles north of Colossae, bounded on the north by a stream of the Lycus River in a steep gorge. Beyond this is the necropolis, with rectangular tombs close together and cut into the rock.

The mound rises some seventy-five feet above the level of the plain, with an acropolis of some 180 by 370 feet, above a larger and lower city. The blocks of stone scattered round the site indicate that future systematic excavation will reveal the shape of the city. Meanwhile relevant inscriptions include two tributes to athletes on altars: one to the winner of a stadium sprint on an altar dedicated to Trajan, another one dedicated to Hadrian. There is a bronze of a young charioteer with a four-horse chariot of Helios (the Sun) dated about A.D. 200, and two fourth-century dedications.

Visitors are advised to approach the site from the main Denizli-Dinar road, taking not the first road marked to Honaz (because of an awkward level-crossing) but rather the second road so marked and some miles further east on the main road. This will bring visitors to the tel, just under a mile short of Honaz. The unexcavated cavea of a small theatre is to be seen on the right at the foot of the tel. This approach affords a very clear view of the magnificent site of Khonai, on a spur above and beyond Honaz. It was during the Byzantine occupation of Colossae that the inhabitants moved to Khonai as more defensible, in the eighth and ninth centuries A.D.

Scripture References:
Colossians (especially 1)
Philemon

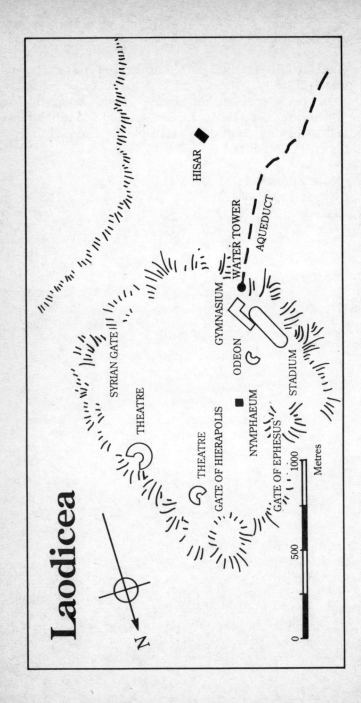

Laodicea

N

Metres

0   500   1000

HISAR

WATER TOWER

AQUEDUCT

GYMNASIUM

ODEON

STADIUM

SYRIAN GATE

THEATRE

THEATRE

GATE OF HIERAPOLIS

NYMPHAEUM

GATE OF EPHESUS

28

LAODICEA

Some time in the reign of the Emperor Domitian at the end of the first century, John the Seer of Patmos – called 'John the Divine' – listed Laodicea last amongst the seven churches of Asia. John reprimanded the Laodiceans for their lukewarmness and lack of enthusiasm. By then, Laodicea was a wealthy city, where Cicero cashed his drafts in 51 B.C. Cicero's speeches include a defence of a Roman governor, Flaccus, who had seized twenty pounds of gold which the Jewish community of Laodicea were sending as an offering to Jerusalem. This huge sum might represent the offerings of some 7,500 freemen, and gives some idea of the size of the Jewish community alone in the city of Laodicea. Following a large earthquake in the year A.D. 60, the city refused help from the senatorial earthquake relief fund in Rome.

The passage in Revelation refers to this and other facts: 'To the angel of the church in Laodicea write: . . . I know your works: you are neither cold nor hot. Would that you were cold or hot! So, because you are lukewarm, and neither cold nor hot, I will spew you out of my mouth [a reference to the emetic qualities of the warm soda/lime water from the hot springs at Hierapolis several miles distant]. For you say, I am rich. I have prospered. I need nothing; not knowing that you are wretched, pitiable, poor, blind and naked . . . Anoint thine eyes with eye-salve that thou mayest see' – a reference to the famous medical school at Laodicea, which pioneered the use of collyrium as an eye ointment, and established a well-known pharmaceutical industry in Roman times.

The amount of time and energy that visitors will expend on this site, which is largely unexcavated and a mile square, will depend upon the heat. It is suggested that, approaching through the village of Eski Hisar and crossing the line of the aqueduct, which is clearly visible coming over the hill from Denizli, visitors should start at the stadium. Passing along the near or west side, the opposite side with its better-preserved seating can be well seen. The best-preserved illustration of what this theatre looked like is now to be seen at Aphrodisias, complete with both subterranean tunnel entrances and surrounding super-structure of arches. At the south end of the stadium is the water tower to which the aqueduct leads. This must be fairly unique; it is a complex of water pipes about twenty feet high. The pipes, like any kettle, have furred up over the centuries and the red pottery of the pipes contrasts with the white calcium deposit. Adjoining, appropriately, both stadium and water supply are the gymnasium and baths. If heat and energy allow, the visitor should walk across the city, eastwards towards Pamukkale, past the odeon and huge nymphaeum – at present under excavation – at the city centre. Continuing to the east edge of the city, he will arrive at a large Greek theatre facing out, on to the Lycus Valley. Turning north he will reach the smaller Roman theatre and join the existing road across the city at the Hierapolis Gate.

Scripture References:
Colossians 2:1
        4:12–18
Revelation 1:11
        3:14–22

29

HIERAPOLIS

The Holy City was depicted on the Roman coinage as a sort of Templeville – a city of many temples. Its greatest characteristic was a series of volcanic springs reaching a temperature of 98°C. These mysterious lime-charged springs could both heal and kill. They were the sites of worship of numerous oriental deities.

The city stands upon neither earth nor rock, but upon a solid calcareous mass deposited through the ages. The process still continues, burying the lower parts of early Roman and Christian buildings to a depth of several feet. The lime deposit forms a self-built limestone channel, which – when it falls over the edge of the plateau – forms a succession of pools and basins, dripping down the cliff in a petrified cascade. From Laodicea, the cascade has the appearance of a 'cotton-wool castle' which is the local name of Hierapolis today.

The hot lime water was well suited to the dye industry. The local goat and sheep wool was dyed purple with local madder root – as it was elsewhere with cochineal and the purple mussel shell – in the second and third centuries A.D.

Hierapolis was built by Antiochus I in the third century B.C. and included within the Roman province of Asia in 129 B.C. The city history was marked by four great earthquakes, the worst of which was in 60 A.D. In the following years – the time of Nero – the city was rebuilt. Successive emperors visited the city: Hadrian in 129, Caracalla in 215, Valens in 370.

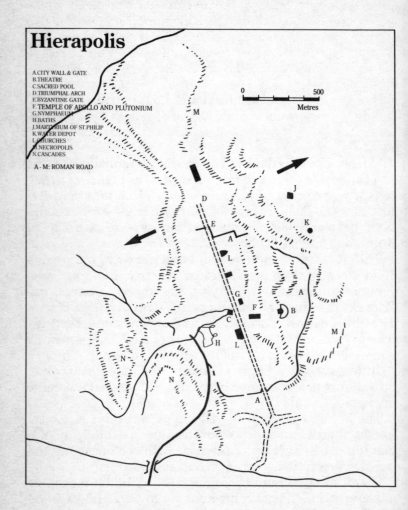

Hierapolis

A. CITY WALL & GATE
B. THEATRE
C. SACRED POOL
D. TRIUMPHAL ARCH
E. BYZANTINE GATE
F. TEMPLE OF APOLLO AND PLUTONIUM
G. NYMPHAEUM
H. BATHS
J. MARTYRIUM OF ST PHILIP
K. WATER DEPOT
L. CHURCHES
N. NECROPOLIS
N. CASCADES

A - M: ROMAN ROAD

0   500

Metres

The surrounding tribes were Phrygian; the constitution first Greek then Roman. The religion was that of the usual Greek gods with some local earlier deities of which the patron was an Apollo, parallel to the Phrygian sun-god whose sanctuary was only twenty miles away north-east of the city; besides Apollo and his mother Leto were Zeus the father, Poseidon of the sea, Pluto of the underworld. An entrance to the underworld – a plutonium – was shown at Hierapolis: a hole under the hill in a fenced enclosure, from which fumes and vapour emerged. It was above this vaporous cave that the Temple of Apollo stood.

The main trades were dyeing and weaving. Guild members listed in inscriptions included a preponderance of Jews. The city prospered from its industries, coppersmiths and marble masons, as well as wool, dye and carpet weavers. The city cemetery from the Hellenistic and Christian periods still numbers 1,200 tombs of which 300 have inscriptions. This necropolis is a mine of information, about the city community, its gladiators, its Jews and Christians. There is a martyrium of St Philip – an octagonal chamber for worship, surrounded by eight chapels. Certainly, Christianity came early to Hierapolis and in the sixth century the Emperor Justinian promoted the Bishop of Hierapolis to Metropolitan of Asia.

An early second century Bishop of Hierapolis, Papias, contributed three important statements for New Testament studies:

1   That Mark wrote Peter's reminiscences of the life and teaching of Jesus, but did not include the *events* in the right order.
2   That Matthew collected and recorded the *sayings* of Jesus in Hebrew and Aramaic. (Was this the gospel or the 'Q' sayings?)
3   That there was another John, 'the Elder', as well as John 'the Apostle'.

Both 1. and 3. are quoted by Eusebius in the fourth century.

Visitors are recommended to start at the north end of the necropolis and, seeking the Greek, Roman and particularly the Jewish motifs among the tombs and sarcophagi, to walk south into the city. The first large building east of the road is a converted Roman baths, whose present 'Chi Ro' motifs on the key stones of the arches show that it was adopted as a Byzantine church. The main *cardo*, or thoroughfare, of the city runs north-south, entering the city by the Gate of Domitian (the emperor during whose persecution John of Patmos was exiled). The ruin of the southern gate, 1,400 yards to the south, still stands at some height.

The theatre has some excellent gladiator and bird reliefs on the proscenium. Little remains of the Temple of Apollo, but a magnificent variety of marble carved pieces and columns is scattered over the site. The fumes from the plutonium have been analysed as carbon dioxide, making the air unbreathable to the height of a man's thigh. Doubtless the priests of the temple could lead animals into the cave for sacrifice and themselves emerge unharmed! The martyrium of Philip is well worth the climb if only for the magnificent view of the whole city.

In order to see the cascades, it is easier to stop your coach or car on the descent from the top, rather than on the climb upwards!

Scripture References:
Colossians 4:13

Part Six:

NON-PAULINE PLACES

Patmos & the Seven Churches of Asia

NEAPOLIS

BYZANTIUM

MACEDONIA

MYSIA

Greece

TROAS

ASSOS

PERGAMUM

THYATIRA

SARDIS

PHILADELPHIA

SMYRNA

HIERAPOLIS

EPHESUS

LAODICEA

COLOSSAE

MILETUS

Patmos

ATTALIA

LYCIA

CNIDUS

PATARA

MYRA

PHOENIX

CRETE

SALMONE

LASEA

CAUDA

0   250

Kilometres

30

JOHN, SEER OF PATMOS AND HIS SEVEN CHURCHES OF ASIA

Some time in the year A.D. 95, during the rule of the Roman Emperor Domitian, a Roman quinquereme – a large galley with five banks of oars – slipped through the surf and spray into the harbour of the rocky island of Patmos. (Patmos is one of a number of small islands off the Turkish coast. From its rocky heights, one can pick out the approximate direction of each of the seven parishes on the mainland.)

While the galley slaves lay exhausted across their oars, a long chain of convicts bound for the Roman penal settlement snaked its way up the rocks to the sound of the lash. These men were shackled and deported for life to work in the stone quarries, sleep in the caves and live in the confines of the island of Patmos.

Among them was one, John, condemned as a Christian agitator for his activities in the seven cities of the mainland, of which the chief was Ephesus. John had made his home at Ephesus and loved his adopted city, having come to speak its language and think in terms of its mentality. He was in origin a Jew baptised a Christian and in heart, but not in soul, a citizen of Ephesus – the cathedral city of paganism in Asia.

Paul the apostle had spent three years – perhaps 54–57 – at the very heart of Greco-Roman civilisation, at Ephesus. Its Temple of Artemis was the centre of pagan pilgrimage for all the Mediterranean world. The proud title of this great commercial and religious centre was 'Neokoros' – temple-

keeper or sacristan of Artemis. Ancient writers considered
that this Benares of the ancient world outshone even the
gardens of Babylon and the Colossus of Rhodes. Its temple
was the focus of a dark, licentious and mysterious oriental
culture, very different from the healthy minded open-air
huntress-goddess known in Greece as Artemis but in Rome
as Diana.

Wherever the deity of a race was female, women took a
prominent part in the life of the place and people. Asia
Minor had been the land of the fabled moon-worshipping
Amazons. Consequently, the Temple of Artemis enjoyed
the services of an army of virgin-prophetesses, eunuch-
priests, choristers, vergers and even acrobats, in a spate of
infamous and immoral excess.

In the early Christian era, Ephesus was a city of magic
and necromancy, the home of a superstition so ancient and
deeply rooted that it outlived the gods of Olympus.

To the little Christian communities founded along the
coastline in the fifties, the Temple of Artemis was an
infernal counterpart to the temple at Jerusalem. A vast
stone staircase led up, past the many-breasted statue of the
Ephesian Artemis to the glistening colonnade and marble
façade. The temple was the size of St Paul's Cathedral in
London, but the same shape and style as the Parthenon in
Athens. White marble colonnades without – dark and
numinous within – contained no cult statue, but a single
colossal meteorite. Paul's letter to the Christian community
at Ephesus declares, 'Once *you* were darkness, but now you
are light *in the Lord*.' First-century coins depict three windows in the high pediment above the façade and four
statues, probably of Amazons, up on the pediment. Pliny
describes 127 marble pillars, each sixty feet high – more
than half of which were overlaid with gold. The high altar,
before the western front of the temple, faced out to sea and
the pilgrims in their thousands crammed the temple courts.

To the worship of Artemis, immensely old and mystical,
was added the modern emperor or 'Caesar-worship' – as a
political expedient in an age that was frankly sceptical of the

old gods. Only two of the emperors took their deity serious-
ly. Caligula, an epileptic and megalomaniac (A.D. 37–41)
insisted on divine honours, even from Jews. But whereas
Caligula was an *in*sane devil, Domitian (A.D. 81–96) was a
sane devil and cold blooded persecutor. Every year, all had
to renew their worship by a pinch of incense on the imperial
altar and the words 'Caesar is Lord'. Christians were con-
fronted with an absolute choice: 'Caesar or Christ'. So, in a
time of mounting terror, John of Patmos, faced with the
savage penal laws 'sacrifice or die', foresaw the fate of his
precious seven mainland parishes, whom he had helped to
found and to grow into Christ. He had had to leave them to
struggle for survival, not only against the ancient evil of
Artemis, but also the modern demands of Caesar. Separated from his beloved parishes by a frustrating narrow
stretch of water, no wonder John's idea of heaven was 'no
more sea' and 'no more thirst'.

Somewhere near to where today the huge fortress
monastery of St John crowns the hilltop – inspired by the
skyscapes and sunsets of Patmos – John wrote the message
of God's denunciation of evil, sending his love, longing and
encouragement to his beloved 'Churches of Asia'. Whereas
the fourth Gospel is written in smooth and correct, if
limited, Greek, the Revelation has no regard for normal
syntax or grammar whatsoever. Perhaps the writer expressed his ecstatic experience *during* his visions and his
intense emotion accounts for his incoherence. The language of his message is so powerful: the crowns, the
thrones, the gold, the colours, the trumpets, the violence,
the pathos. Monsters lurk and glories blaze, as with surrealistic artistry, John stirs our subconscious minds. In the
compulsion of his visions, the 'silence in heaven' is intoler-
able, and 'the single eagle flying in mid-air' mewing in pity
for the inhabitants of the earth is unbearably poignant, and
'the leaves of the Tree of Life are for the healing of the
nations'.

Here on Patmos, in his cave cell or on the hilltop, John,
seer and convict of the stone quarries, alternately opened

the door into heaven and lifted the cover off the bottomless pit. Living in an age of blood and fire, not a vindictive man, he wrote 'in the spirit', with a frightening sense of the reality of good and evil – a reality whose bitterness burns, but whose sweetness is inexpressible.

'He who testifies to these things says: "Surely I am coming soon." Amen, come, Lord Jesus.'

Scripture References:
Revelation (especially 1, 7, 21, 22:16–21)

31

CAPPADOCIA – AN INTRODUCTION: THE PLACES

We spend three nights in Cappadocia, based on Urgup, from which we explore this remarkable region of natural, religious and cultural interest. In the heart of the Anatolian plateau, bounded by the cities of Aksaray, Kayseri and Nigde, lies this strange and spellbinding landscape – unique in the world.

Successive eruptions of the now extinct volcanoes of Erciyas Dag and Hasan Dag have left the plateau covered in volcanic tuff. This soft rock has been transformed by intense erosion into a haunting, surrealistic landscape of caves, columns and canyons. Oxidisation of the rock has turned this weird world into an array of colours from warm reds and golds to cool greens and greys.

Cappadocia is more than an area of dramatic natural beauty. For 1,000 years, from the fourth to the thirteenth century, Christians cut chapels and houses in the rock. The architecture is totally incorporated into the landscape. The rich ochre-toned Byzantine paintings seem to reflect the colours of the surrounding landscape. Most of the frescoes are the fruit of popular art without concern for aesthetics or real artistic creation. While painting, the artists – mostly monks in monastic colonies – followed the impulse of their religious feelings or convictions, rather than any actual artistic inspiration.

The oldest frescoes show connections with Palestinian and Syrian art, which inherited traditions going back to

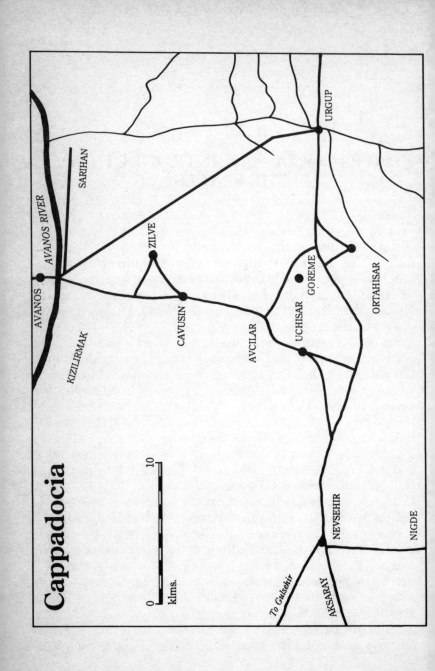

Cappadocia

AVANOS RIVER

AVANOS

KIZILIRMAK

SARIHAN

ZILVE

CAVUSIN

AVCILAR

UCHISAR

GOREME

ORTAHISAR

URGUP

NEVSEHIR

NIGDE

AKSARAY

To Gulsehir

0   10
klms.

the earliest centuries of the Christian era. Others were influenced by Byzantine art and in turn Byzantium, particularly during the fourteenth century, received oriental artistic contributions from Cappadocia.

The monastic colonies long outlived the Seljuk and Ottoman conquests. It is impossible to give exact dates for the building of each chapel or church, but some inscriptions and dedications remain. The period during which Cappadocia flourished as an important Christian monastic centre lasted from the ninth to the thirteenth centuries. Since when, it has remained a zone of historical fusion between eastern and western cultures with Byzantine churches alongside the magnificent mosques, medresses (seminaries) and caravanserais of the Seljuk and Ottoman Turks.

Urgup is a picturesque village at the foot of a cliff, riddled with troglodyte dwellings, more or less in the centre of our area of exploration. Though distances between sites are small, there is much to see and time will limit us to a selection best known to our guide. The most accessible and interesting are the Rock Churches of the Goreme Valley.

A characteristic group of the Byzantine pattern, cruciform in shape but having lost their screens or iconastases – is made up of the following:

1   *CARIKLI Kilisi, 'Church of the Sandals'*
    So-called from the footprints scooped out of the ground in the south transept – under a picture of the Ascension – reminiscent of the footsteps in the sanctuary of the Ascension on the Mount of Olives!

    The main paintings are: the Nativity, the Crucifixion, the Ascension and 'The Hospitality of Abraham', perhaps the best preserved of any within this group of churches. Note the disproportionate size of the portraits to the rest of the picture.

    The entrance is at the end of the northern transept. The cruciform shape is outlined by a central cupola with semi-circular vaults on three sides and a small cupola over the eastern area. There are two columns, three altars against the walls and a seat in each apse. A bench runs along part of the nave and there are two graves in the floor.

2 *KARANLIK Kilisi, 'The Dark Church'*
Lit only by a small window in the narthex. Owing to the exclusion of light, its paintings are in a good state of preservation. The ornamentation is rich and varied. The church, built in the side of a rock face, a few yards above ground level, has a rectangular narthex, reached by a spiral staircase and a naos built on four columns, flanked by a triple apse. The narthex is transversal to the church and there is a burial chamber with three graves.

There is a chapel scooped out of the rock between these two churches (the 'Sandals' and the 'Dark'). An arch over the door is decorated with a cross within a medallion. The chapel is formed by two crosses, the narthex or entrance and the chapel – undecorated but with graves.

3 *KARANLIK, Monastery and Refectory*
A monastery on two floors was near the 'Dark' church. A series of blind arcades is all that remains of the façade. The long ground-floor vestibule has lost its front wall. The upper-floor arcades are decorated with white Maltese crosses in red medallions. Three independent halls open off the vestibule. On the upper floor, there is a long room at the front and two halls at the back. The refectory was cut out *after* the church. The hall is twenty-seven feet long and fourteen feet wide. On the left stands the only remaining table with a bench round it, following the outline of the apse to form a seat of honour for the abbot. This is reminiscent of dining halls at Mount Athos and St Saba monasteries.

4 *ELMALI Kilisi, 'The Apple Church'*
Built much later than the others, the smallest of the columned churches. Bright decoration and vivid colours make it most attractive. Built in an isolated rock pillar, at the end of a circle of cliffs. The narthex has gone; the church is similar in shape to the 'Dark' church. All its columns have been preserved and stand on square

bases. There are three apses with seats on the right side. A low bench runs all round the chapel. The walls and pilasters are ornamented with chequered stripes. Zigzag patterns decorate the bases of the arches and cupolas. There are both medallions and Latin crosses.

5   *BARBARA Kilisi, 'Church of St Barbara'*
Built in the same rock as the 'Apple' church, but at a higher level, with the door on the south side. Three panels of saints on the wall. Facing the door are St Theodorus and St George. At the end of the west arm of the cross is St Barbara. These and the Christ, within the apse, are later than the church itself. The coarse red ochre decoration has been added at various periods.

6   *YILANLI Kilisi, 'Church of the Snakes'*
Nearby.

7   *TOKALI Kilisi, 'Church of the Buckle'*
The largest of the group with well-preserved frescoes throughout. New Testament scenes from the Annunciation to the Ascension. Over 100 pictures of the saints, including a sequence from the life of St Basil – of different periods.

   Built in a large rock pillar only yards from the Urgup road, the church includes (built at different periods):
   - an irregular vestibule, part destroyed, giving access to
   - a small undecorated hall (on the left) and through a large arch to
   - the church:
     the nave, sixteen feet long, roughly rectangular;
     an upper hall, thirty feet long;
     four thick pillars joined by arches;
     a chapel with a nave thirteen feet long.

BEYOND THE GOREME VALLEY

The following are of the greatest interest (see map outline):
   Avcilar: seat of a Byzantine bishop; a picturesque

semi-troglodyte village with houses attached
to rock cones, called 'fairy chimneys'.

Cavusin: on the road to Avanos; a village beside a cliff
honeycombed with grottoes. At the top is the
church of St John the Baptist.

Zilve: north-east of Cavusin; a fantastic troglodyte
site, a mass of Byzantine chapels and dwellings with red rock cones.

Avanos: on the River Kizilirmak; famous for onyx
ware, pottery and carpets.

Uchisar: a village around a striking rock pinnacle,
affording a spectacular view of the surrounding erosion basin.

Ortahisar: a village at the foot of a rock honeycombed
with caves. Nearby is Balkan Deresi and more
rock churches.

Ihlara: a deep scenic canyon with many churches, set
in a beautiful pastoral valley.

Scripture References:
Acts 2:1–11
1 Peter 1:1 and 2

32

CAPPADOCIA – THE PEOPLE

Cappadocia has played a unique part in the history and doctrine of the Christian Church. There were visitors from Cappadocia at Pentecost. St Peter wrote to Jewish converts in Cappadocia (1 Pet. 1:1). In the early years of the fourth century, a pastor in Alexandria, Egypt, called Arius, expressed his belief in Christ as a hybrid – half god and half man. This heresy spread fast, but was opposed by Athanasius, Bishop of Alexandria in the year 328 on the grounds that a hybrid could neither reveal God nor save man. Athanasius suffered five exiles, such were the fierce theological and political quarrels with the Arian heresy. He was one of the most decisive thinkers in Christian history and the champion of the *eternal divinity* of Christ. At times the Arians even had the Emperor Constantine on their side, but Athanasius was a courageous and resourceful man of action as well as a brilliant thinker.

On 20 May 325, at Nicea on the coast 100 miles south-west of Istanbul, Constantine presided at the first 'ecumenical council' of the Christian Church attended by some 220 bishops. That council approved a creed affirming the total equality of Father, Son and Spirit and declaring Christ to be '*of one substance*' with the Father. Today, you and I recite the *Apostle's* Creed at morning and evening service and the *Nicene* Creed at communion, without always registering the difference! Some of us notice that the Nicene Creed is an expansion of the Apostle's Creed to clarify the teaching of the Trinity. Have we who now use

the Alternative Service Book noticed how the Nicene Creed
has been newly worded thus?

> We believe in one Lord, Jesus Christ,
> the only Son of God.
> *Eternally begotten* of the Father
> God *from* God, Light *from* Light,
> True God *from* True God
> begotten, not made,
> *of one Being with the Father*.

Athanasius died in 373, but the doctrinal battle for the
completeness of Christ's humanity continued. The mantle of
Athanasius passed to a trio of men called 'The Cappadocian
Fathers'. Each of them was an important theologian of the
Eastern Orthodox Church and a bishop of that Church,
here in Cappadocia. To them, we owe the survival of the
Nicene Creed and of the affirmation of 'three *persons* in one
God'. These three were Basil the Great, Bishop of Caesarea
(now Kayseri), the metropolis of Cappadocia, Gregory
(Basil's younger brother), Bishop of Nyssa (now near
Aydin) and another Gregory (friend of Basil), Bishop of
Sasina (up the road) and Nazianzas in Constantinople.

Some of their thinking and their 'fighting' for a true faith
in the Trinity is reflected in what is called the 'Athanasian
Creed', printed after matins and evensong in the Book of
Common Prayer.

Basil the Great, from Cappadocia, was recognised as the
encourager and regulator of monasticism in the east.
Pagans complained that when he came to Cappadocia,
there were seventeen Christians in the region and when he
died there were only seventeen pagans. He lived at a time
when Christian hermits escaped from the world by ex-
cessive austerity and discipline and were venerated and
respected by other Christians for their self-denial. Basil
realised that if one cut oneself off completely from human
society, it was impossible to fulfil the gospel of charity, to
comfort and care for others.

He changed the military discipline of rigid monasticism into a kind of family organisation. He regulated monastic life into periods of prayer, study and manual labour, linking it with the organisation of charity. Here in Cappadocia, religious communities began to include hospitals, homes for the poor and schools for children. At Caesarea (up the road) the city gathered around the monastic centre. These monasteries acted as bastions of orthodoxy holding the whole community against the invasion of false teachings.

The Liturgy of Basil the Great is still in regular use within the Orthodox Church. Some of his prayers may help us to understand the Christianity of those who lived and worshipped in this strange landscape of Cappadocia:

PRAYER TO THE MOST HOLY TRINITY
Arising from sleep I thank thee, O Holy Trinity, that, for the sake of thy great kindness and long-suffering, thou hast not had indignation against me, for I am slothful and sinful, neither hast thou destroyed me in my transgressions: but thou hast raised me up as I lay in heedlessness, that I might sing my morning hymn and glorify thy sovreignty. Do thou now enlighten the eyes of my understanding, open my ears to receive thy words and teach me thy commandments. Help me to do thy will, to hymn thee, to confess thee from my heart, and to extol thine All-holy Name, of Father, Son and Holy Ghost, now and for ever, and unto the ages of ages. Amen.

O come, let us worship God, our King.

O come, let us worship and fall down before Christ, our King and our God.

O come, let us worship and fall down before Christ, our King and our God.

PRAYER OF REPENTANCE

O Lord and Master, Jesus Christ, our God, the well of life and of immortality, the Maker of every thing visible and invisible, the co-eternal and co-everlasting Father, who for the abundance of his goodness, in these latter days, didst put on flesh and wast crucified and buried for us unthankful and ungracious men, and hast by thy own blood renewed our nature corrupted by sin: do thou, O immortal King, accept the repentance of me, a sinner, and incline thine ear to me, and hearken to my words. Amen.

PRAYER BEFORE COMMUNION

I know, O Lord, that I partake unworthily of thy pure Body and of thy precious Blood, and am guilty, and eat and drink condemnation to myself, not discerning thy Body and Blood, my Christ and my God: yet emboldened by thy loving-kindnesses I come to thee, who hast said, He that eateth my Flesh and drinketh my Blood, abideth in me and I in him. Be pitiful, therefore, O Lord, and put me not to rebuke, a sinner, but deal with me according to thy mercy. And let these holy things afford me healing and cleansing; enlightenment and protection; sanctification of soul and body and the averting of every fantasy, evil practice and operation of the devil, which of design worketh in my members. Let them give me confidence and love towards thee; amendment of life, and perseverance; increase of virtue and perfection; fulfilment of thy commandments; fellowship of the Holy Spirit; provision for the journey of eternal life; and an acceptable answer at thy dread judgment-seat; but not judgment or condemnation. Amen.

PRAYER AFTER COMMUNION

O Christ, Master and God, King of the ages, Maker of all things, I thank thee for all the good gifts thou hast given me, and especially for the participation in thy pure and life-giving mysteries. I pray thee, therefore, gracious Lord that lovest all men, preserve me under thy protection and beneath the shadow of thy wings; and grant me, even to my last breath, to partake worthily and with a pure conscience of thy holy things, unto remission of sins and unto life eternal. For thou art the bread of life, the well of holiness, the river of all good: and to thee we ascribe glory, with the Father and the Holy Spirit, now and for ever, and unto the ages of ages. Amen.

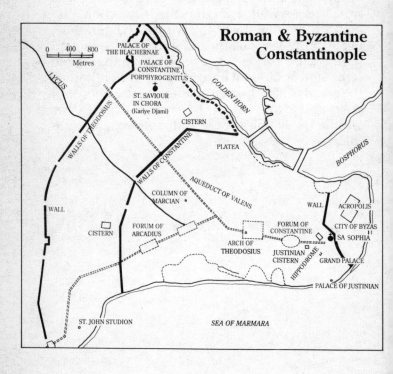

Roman & Byzantine Constantinople

PALACE OF THE BLACHERNAE

PALACE OF CONSTANTINE PORPHYROGENITUS

0 400 800
Metres

LYCUS

GOLDEN HORN

BOSPHORUS

WALLS OF THEODOSIUS

WALLS OF CONSTANTINE

ST. SAVIOUR IN CHORA
(Kariye Djami)

CISTERN

PLATEA

AQUEDUCT OF VALENS

COLUMN OF MARCIAN

WALL

ACROPOLIS

CISTERN

FORUM OF ARCADIUS

FORUM OF CONSTANTINE

CITY OF BYZAS

SA SOPHIA

ARCH OF THEODOSIUS

JUSTINIAN CISTERN

HIPPODROME

GRAND PALACE

WALL

PALACE OF JUSTINIAN

ST. JOHN STUDION

SEA OF MARMARA

33

ISTANBUL

LYGOS

The city is divided into three urban areas today, by the Bosphorus waterway, the Golden Horn inlet and the Sea of Marmara. From 4000 B.C., the Bosphorus was a busy thoroughfare, many peoples passing through the straits from eastern Europe to Asia, particularly during the fall of the Hittite empire in the thirteenth century B.C. The first settlement on the Golden Horn was established about that time and later moved to the present Seraglio Point where, according to Pliny the Younger, there was already a fishermen's village of Lygos.

BYZANTIUM

In the seventh century B.C., a Greek sailor named Byzas, from Megara on the Isthmus of Corinth, founded a town which bore his name, Byzantium. Before doing so, he consulted the Delphic oracle as to where he should settle and received the enigmatic answer 'opposite the blind'. Other Megarians had previously settled on the Asian side of the Bosphorus facing the Golden Horn. Byzas interpreted the oracle to mean that his fellow countrymen were blind not to have realised the advantages of the natural harbour of the Horn. He himself settled on the promontory of Lygos where, thanks to the shelter of the inlet and his easily defensible position, Byzantium soon became a big trading centre.

After successive occupations by Darius of Persia, Pausanias of Sparta, and Philip of Macedon – father of Alexander the Great – Byzantium negotiated a truce and commercial agreement with the Gauls, the last invaders. It was in thanksgiving to the moon, which revealed Philip of Macedon's night attack, that the sign of the crescent moon became the symbol of Byzantium.

AUGUSTA ANTONIA

Weakened by continuous warfare, Byzantium fell at last to the Roman legions. During the last century B.C., Byzantium declared itself for Rome and was rewarded by Roman protection and privilege, being made a Roman province by the Emperor Vespasian. For a hundred years of Pax Romana, the city prospered until it unwisely backed Prescennius Niger against Septimus Severus. After a long and bloody siege, Septimus Severus captured, punished and rebuilt the city, adding many public buildings to mark his victory, renaming the city Augusta Antonia in 196 A.D.

NEW ROME

Constantine's rival, Licinius, fled to Byzantium, settling on the Asian bank of the Bosphorus, where Constantine caught up with him in 324. The city, surrounded by siege towers, capitulated without resistance. Constantine soon realised the strategic and commercial potential of the position of the city. He decided to make it the capital of the Roman empire, giving it the name New Rome. He himself traced the extended perimeter of the new city, enclosing a huge triangle between the Golden Horn and the Marmara. The emperor built the imperial palace, forum, senate and first Sa Sophia, enlarging the hippodrome and adding to

the acropolis. The new capital was inaugurated in 330 and
the emperor moved into his palace.

CONSTANTINOPLE

For the next fifty years Christianity and paganism were
officially practised side by side. It was Theodosius the Great
who wiped out the final traces of paganism. On his death
his two sons divided the empire, west and east, based on
Rome and Byzantium – henceforth known as Constantinople. On the fall of Rome to the barbarians in 476, Constantinople became the centre of the civilised world. But, for the
next fifty years, the empire suffered from intrigues, plagues
and fires, civil wars and barbarian invasions. In 1553 the
Circus riots brought about the destruction of the Sa Sophia,
the senate and baths of Septimus Severus.

JUSTINIAN'S GOLDEN AGE

The Emperor Justinian's marriage to the 'actress and harlot'
Theodora finally united the warring factions in the city.
Justinian rebuilt the whole city and the Sa Sophia, as it
stands today. He repelled the Vandals, Goths and Persians
and set up an authoritative and enlightened government
which fostered the golden age of Constantinople and the
climax of Byzantine civilisation.

Having reached a zenith under Justinian and Theodora,
the power of Constantinople soon waned. Waves of in-
vading barbarians, Persians and Arabs overran the land,
flowing to the foot of the great walls of the city itself. Four
times the Arabs besieged Constantinople by land and sea,
always repulsed by 'Greek fire', a napalm-like preparation
(used in grenade and mortar form) which destroyed the
Arab fleet in 672.

The emperors conducted a campaign against the Church,
jealous of its power over the people. The city was torn in

two, particularly by the imperial condemnation of the veneration of holy images. Thousands of works of art of all kinds were hunted down and destroyed.

In the ninth century another Theodora, ruling as regent for her son, restored the cult of images – in the process hanging, decapitating and burning 100,000 Manichean heretics.

MACEDONIAN GOLDEN AGE

In 867 the Emperor Basil I established a Macedonian dynasty which was to survive until 1067. Under the Macedonian emperors, the city became the centre of a great political and religious empire once more. The pomp and sophistication of the court were unequalled. Byzantine art was supreme in both east and west. The city enjoyed a second golden age in the reign of the Emperor Constantine Porphyrogenetus, 912–959. However, the rise in the arts of peace and effeminate refinement led to a weakening of ruling power. Within the Church, the dogmatic dispute over the 'filioque' clause was overlaid with quibbling and bickering. Constantinople could not accept Rome's religious supremacy, having won the political leadership. Mutual excommunications followed and, where there had been two empires, there were now two Churches.

CRUSADES

From the time of Justinian, Venetians, Amalfans and Genoese had settled in Galata (north of the Golden Horn). The religious schism was bound to aggravate the fundamental enmity between these people of Latin origin and the native Greek population. Conflict was inevitably sparked off by the Crusades, yet the first Crusade passed by the city in 1097 and the second Crusade in 1147. Even the third Crusade avoided the city, though by now the Latin nobles were carving out neat little kingdoms for themselves and the emperors were demanding restitution of all filched lands.

LATIN EMPIRE

Ultimately, faction within the city itself resulted in an invitation to the leaders of the fourth Crusade to restore a dethroned emperor. Attracted by the proverbial wealth of the city, an army of 40,000 Crusaders took the city, in 1203, and crowned the emperor who accepted reconciliation with the papacy, in return for services rendered. The Greek population promptly revolted and assassinated the emperor, whereupon the Crusaders returned the following year to pillage and occupy the city. Baldwin of Flanders was crowned Latin Emperor of the Orient by the Papal Legate and the empire divided up between the Frankish barons. Within fifty years the Latin empire was gradually being recaptured by the Greeks, as in turn their possessions in Asia and Europe were being taken over by the Turks. The Ottoman conquest had begun.

OTTOMAN CONQUEST

Having consumed the Abbasids of Baghdad, the Turks migrated west over the Caucasus into Anatolia, taking Nicaea and Adrianople, Thessaly and Macedonia. Early in 1452 Mehmet II (the Conqueror) landed on the European side of the Bosphorus, where he built the castle of Rumeli Hisar, opposite that of Anadolu Hisar on the Asian side. The Emperor Constantine XI repaired the city walls and hung a chain across the Golden Horn to prevent all ships entering. The siege began on 5 April; 80,000 Turks surrounding 20,000 Greeks and others.

During the night of 23 April, the Sultan had part of his fleet taken overland from the Bosphorus to the Golden

Horn. From there he bombarded the sea walls of the Golden Horn and cut all communications between the city and Galata. To do this, seventy galleys were dragged on greased planks along a track four to five miles long. The Greeks tried to set fire to the galleys, but all other vessels in the Golden Horn inlet were sunk. All conditions of surrender were rejected. The emperor was killed in action. The sultan returned on horseback and took possession of the Sa Sophia, which he ordered to be converted into a mosque, surmounted by the star and crescent. The crescent came from old Byzantium, the star from the sultan himself. The new name Istanbul is a corruption of *eis tēn polin* (literally into the city) from the Greek signs to the city centre.

Once the town was taken, killings ceased and Islam showed more mercy in victory than Christianity. The sultan allowed many Christian groups to return and settle round their patriarchates and churches – including the Greeks in the Fener. Within three centuries, the population grew from 60,000 to 500,000. In 1914 the Turks took sides with Germany. Defeat brought the Ottoman empire to an end and Istanbul was occupied by the Allies from 1918 to 1923.

ATATURK

Mustafa Kemal, called Ataturk – father of Turks – led a national revolution to found a young, prosperous and dynamic democracy on the lines of the Ottoman empire. The Treaty of Lausanne, signed on 24 November 1923, confirmed the victory of Ataturk's government. The republic of Turkey was proclaimed on 29 October, with Ankara as capital, and Ataturk as president. Since then, this great historical and artistic city has prospered as the gateway between east and west.

THE BLUE MOSQUE

Mosque of Sultan Ahmet I built 1609–17 and known as the 'Blue Mosque' because this colour dominates the decoration. A perfect square with a great dome and four half domes supported by four massive columns. The lower walls of the prayer hall and gallery retain the original tiles with the traditional designs of lily, carnation, tulip, rose, cypress and other trees. The painting in the dome and on the upper walls is a modern copy of the original. The white marble mihrab (niche indicating the direction of Mecca) and minbar (pulpit) are part of the original furnishing.

The square beside the mosque is the ancient hippodrome and the surrounding roads follow the original chariot track. Begun by Septimus Severus; rebuilt and enlarged by Constantine and said to seat 100,000 spectators. The Egyptian obelisk erected here in A.D. 390 by Theodosius the Great is one of a pair that Thutmose III (1490–1436 B.C.) placed in the great temple of Karnak. The scenes on the base show the emperor and his family presiding over the races as well as the erection of the obelisk. The Serpentine Column was brought from the Temple of Apollo at Delphi.

SA SOPHIA (Church of the Holy Wisdom)

The third church on this site, built by Justinian and dedicated in A.D. 537. Though restored several times in the Byzantine and Ottoman periods, what we see today is essentially the work of Justinian. The major additions are external, huge buttresses of 1317 (restored by Sinan in the sixteenth century) and minarets of various dates after the conversion to a mosque in 1453. The vast nave, 100 feet wide, with a great dome and half domes is flanked by aisles and galleries. Many of the columns were brought from ancient temples. The sumptuous decoration has been removed except for some fine mosaics:

1　Above the entrance:
　　Constantine and Justinian with Virgin and Child, tenth
　　century.
2　In narthex (lunette above central door):
　　Enthroned Christ with an emperor, tenth century.
3　North Gallery:
　　Full length portrait of Emperor Alexander, ninth cen-
　　tury.
4　South Gallery:
　　Christ with the Virgin and St John the Baptist, four-
　　teenth century.
　　Constantine IX and Empress Zoe, eleventh century.
　　John II and his wife Irene presenting gifts to the Virgin
　　and Child.
5　Apse:
　　Virgin and Child, ninth century.
In the garden to the south of the church are the tombs of five
sultans, that of Selim II (d. 1574) by Sinan, and in the garden
to the west are architectural remains from excavations
around the city.

TOPKAPI PALACE

Standing on the site of the acropolis of ancient Byzantium
this charming collection of courts, gardens and pavilions
was the residence of the Ottoman sultans from the time of
Mehmet II (1451–81) until 1853. It has been a museum since
1924 and houses a magnificent collection of porcelain,
miniatures, tapestries, imperial costume, jewellery and
precious objects belonging to the sultans. Also relics of
Muhammed. The Archeological Museum contains two
unique exhibits from Jerusalem: the Siloam Stone, from
the conduit, and the only surviving warning notice from
the Gentiles Courtyard balustrade in the Herodian Temple.

SULEIMANIYE MOSQUE

Built for Suleiman the Magnificent by Sinan 1550–57, it is the most sumptuous of the imperial mosques. The prayer hall is a variation of Sa Sophia with a central dome and two half domes supported by four large columns, with five domes in each aisle. There is much carved wood with ivory and mother-of-pearl inlay and the windows have beautiful Ottoman stained glass. Beyond the courtyard are many buildings which were part of the complex – schools, hospital, medical college and caravanserai. The tombs of Suleiman and his wife are behind the mosque.

CHURCH OF THE HOLY SAVIOUR-IN-CHORA

The second most important Byzantine monument in the city with a superb collection of mosaics. Most of the church dates from the time of Justinian (527–565), of rather unusual design with two narthexes and a nave without side aisles. The six groups of mosaics deal with the life of Christ and the Blessed Virgin. They are:

Outer narthex:
  Christ Pantocrator.
  The Virgin with Angels.
  Theodore Metochites presenting his Church to Christ.
  Saints Peter and Paul.
  Christ with the Virgin and St John the Baptist.
  The Infancy of Christ.
  Christ's Ministry.
Inner narthex:
  Genealogy of Christ (domes).
  Life of the Blessed Virgin.
Nave:
  Dormition of the Virgin.
  Christ holding the Gospels.
  The Virgin Hodeghetria (guide or teacher).

Frescoes in the Parecclesion (mortuary chapel on south side):
  The Resurrection and the Life.
  The Last Judgment.
  Heaven and Hell.
  The Mother of God as the bridge between Earth and Heaven.

INDEX OF PLACES AND PEOPLE

PAUL

Günther Bornkamm

Paul is a scholarly and well informed look at the life and travels of the greatest of Apostles. Drawing on the New Testament records (in the Acts of the Apostles and the Pauline letters) as well as non-biblical sources, Günther Bornkamm examines Paul's ideas and beliefs in detail. Theme by theme he unravels the Pauline views originally written in letters directed to particular places and circumstances. He concludes by addressing himself to the 'Jesus and Paul' question. Did Paul promote without change, or corrupt and betray the message and intent of Jesus?

'Bornkamm's reconstruction of the life and work of Paul is a fine piece of scholarly work, but his exposition of the apostle's gospel and theology in the second part of the book is superb . . . He shows how ill-founded is the common view (which has found expression from Paul's time to ours) that Paul perverted the message of Jesus. Paul, on the contrary, inherited the mind of Jesus in rare degree.'

F. F. Bruce

COME, SEE THE PLACE

Ronald Brownrigg

A revised and expanded edition of this much acclaimed travel-guide to the Holy Land with up-to-date practical information, details of recent archaeological discoveries and sixteen pages of colour photographs.

'A unique combination of devotional and practical.'

Mowbrays Journal

'It is the best-informed and most comprehensive of all the many Holy Land guidebooks that have come my way, and I found it hard to put down . . . admirable maps and illustrations add greatly to the interest.'

Church Times

'This pilgrim's guide will awaken each visitor's awareness of the events which took place within those sacred surroundings, and help them discover the presence of the Spirit of the Living Christ who is "the same yesterday, today and forever".'

Church of England Newspaper

'This book is packed with routes, maps, sightseeing tips and details of transport and accessibility.'

Christian Woman

Canon Brownrigg has been a frequent visitor to the Holy Land for over forty years, and is the author of numerous books, including *Who's Who in the New Testament*.

THE HODDER BIBLE HANDBOOK

Merrill Unger & Gary Larson

An indispensable guide to the study of the Bible, this is three books in one: commentary, atlas and encyclopaedia.

* detailed book-by-book Bible commentary
* 500 full-colour illustrations and photographs
* 70 colour maps and charts
* easy to use chapter and verse reference system
* 40 special subjects include archaeology, geography, weights and measures, historical and cultural background to the Old Testament, and a summary of church history
* keyed to the New International Version, but suitable for use with all Bible versions
* focuses on the spiritual application of the Bible's message

'The commentary is of a particularly high quality – concise enough for the needs of the reader 'dipping in', yet sufficient attention to detail to satisfy more systematic study of the Bible.'

Baptist Times

PAUL
Portrait of a Revolutionary

Donald Coggan

Paul – tireless pilgrim, bold church founder and inspiring leader – was a man continually on the road. Lord Coggan has retraced the steps of the great apostle to write his illuminating story of the man who is 'truly one of us' in our sorrows, fears and joys.

'With many an apt quotation from writers of imagination, the book is lively and informative, even for those who may think they have met this Revolutionary before.'

Catholic Herald

Donald Coggan was Archbishop of Canterbury from 1974 to 1980.